Dvořák

His Life and Music

www.naxos.com/naxosbooks/dvoraklifeandmusic

by Neil Wenborn

Dvořák

His Life and Music

For Susan and Colin
a wedding present

Author's Acknowledgements

This book draws on several sources for translations of Dvořák's correspondence, contemporary accounts and other primary material. The author and publishers gratefully acknowledge the originators of these translations, the sources of which are listed in the bibliography. I would also like to thank Genevieve Helsby of Naxos Books for suggesting the project and for seeing it through to completion, and Anthony Short, whose editorial vigilance and sensitivity have been enormously reassuring. My greatest debt of gratitude is, as ever, to Sue and Edward, who have borne patiently with Dvořák as a long-staying house-guest.

Published by Naxos Books, an imprint of Naxos Rights International Ltd

© Naxos Books 2008

www.naxosbooks.com

Printed and bound in China by Leo Paper Group

Design and layout: Hannah Davies, Fruition – Creative Concepts

All photographs © Lebrecht Music & Arts Photo Library

Edited by Anthony Short

Front cover background picture: The National Theatre, Prague

A CIP Record for this book is available from the British Library.

ISBN: 978-1-84379-116-4

Contents

www.naxos.com/naxosbooks/dvoraklifeandmusic

Visit the dedicated website for *Dvořák: His Life and Music* and gain free access to the following:

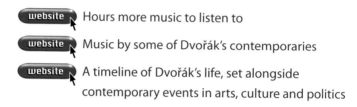

Hours more music to listen to

Music by some of Dvořák's contemporaries

A timeline of Dvořák's life, set alongside contemporary events in arts, culture and politics

To access this you will need:

- ISBN: 9781843791164
- Password: Dumky

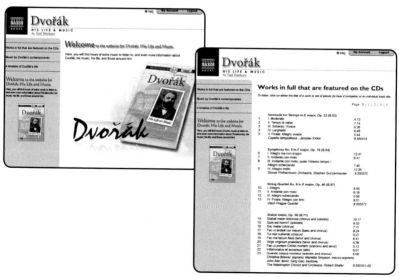

www.naxos.com/naxosbooks/dvoraklifeandmusic

Preface

Dvořák is one of that select handful of classical composers who can claim near-universal recognition. His 'New World' Symphony stands among the hardy perennials of the repertoire, the theme of its slow movement almost as widely known as the opening of Beethoven's Fifth. In the United States it has been set to words as a spiritual, while for a generation of television viewers in Britain it is inseparable from the image of a young boy trudging home up a hill with a loaf of Hovis. The music's appeal transcends geographical, cultural and even, on one historic occasion, terrestrial boundaries. The work of a Czech composer living in America, it is particularly popular in Japan; and when Neil Armstrong and Buzz Aldrin landed on the moon in 1969 they carried a cassette of the 'New World' Symphony with them in the lunar module.

The 'New World' is only the most visible face of Dvořák's extraordinarily multifaceted achievement. Behind it lies one of the most remarkable oeuvres of the second half of the nineteenth century. Antonín Dvořák was both the most prolific and the most versatile of the late Romantic masters. The catalogue of his original works compiled by the Czech musicologist and composer Jarmil Burghauser runs to more than 200 items. (Burghauser's numbering, designated B.1 etc., is a more reliable guide to the order of composition than the notoriously arbitrary opus numbering used by Dvořák and his publishers.) Almost every major classical form except the piano sonata is represented in this astonishing body of work. In a creative career lasting more than forty years Dvořák wrote nine symphonies, four concertos, several symphonic poems, rhapsodies and other orchestral works (including the immensely popular *Slavonic Dances*), fourteen string quartets, four extant piano trios, a series of major sacred and secular choral works, and ten operas – not to mention music for a myriad of other chamber combinations, as well as numerous songs and keyboard compositions. Many of these works are among the staples of the modern concert platform and recording studio; only the operas – ironically the form by which the composer himself set the greatest store – have been slow to make their presence felt outside his native land.

Yet at the same time Dvořák is so completely a product of the Czech lands that, almost uniquely among composers, he is by far his country's best-known son. Wagner may, for baneful reasons, be indelibly associated with a period in his country's history; Mozart, for highly questionable ones, with a chocolate-box image of his. But neither stands unrivalled as the international face of his homeland in the way that Dvořák does for the Czech lands. Among Bohemia's many cultural exports over the centuries, perhaps only Good King Wenceslas has achieved equivalent currency.

A profoundly national musician, then, Antonín Dvořák was also the first and greatest internationalist in his country's musical history. The paradox is one of several in the composer's life and work. For the listener, his characteristic musical gift is spontaneity, the 'heavenly naturalness' of melodic invention remarked by so many reviewers, both in his own time and since. Yet Dvořák was the most conscious and self-critical of craftsmen, and his sketchbooks are testimony to the arduous workings and difficulties – what he called the 'knots' – behind the seemingly easy flow of the music we now hear. He is the sunniest and most accessible of the late Romantics, yet some of his greatest works – the F minor Piano Trio, the Seventh Symphony – are among the most anguished ever written. The closer one looks, the more the paradoxes accumulate. His older contemporary, Bedřich Smetana (the so-called 'father of Czech music') was in many ways the more cosmopolitan figure; yet it was Dvořák, with his deeply conservative peasant roots, who brought that music to the attention of the world. It was Dvořák, too, who like a gruff colossus, straddled the rift in the musical landscape created by the opposing polarities of Wagner and Brahms; he remained at once a passionate Wagnerian and a devoted personal friend of Brahms, while the two most vehement partisans of this musical controversy, Hans Richter and Eduard Hanslick, were both among his staunchest supporters.

As with the music, so with the man. Dvořák liked to portray himself as 'a simple Czech musician', an image he cultivated, more or less consciously, throughout his career. The reality was far more complex. Dvořák's personality inevitably remains elusive, but his sometimes disconcerting eccentricities – the extreme absent-mindedness, the unpredictability of temper, the taciturnity broken by outbursts of childlike enthusiasm, the rigid inflexibility of his personal habits – may well suggest some psychological turmoil at the root of his restless creativity. A countryman by birth and inclination, he spent much of his life in cities, where he was so afflicted by nervous phobias that he seldom went out alone: one friend recalled how, at Dvořák's urgent entreaty, he once accompanied him to a café, only for the composer to ignore his every conversational overture until it was time to leave, at which point Dvořák jumped up, seized him by the hand and thanked him effusively. A deeply private and undemonstrative man, he nonetheless had one of the highest public profiles of any contemporary musician (including, in New York in the 1890s, that of trailblazer for American music), and his visits to England generated the kind of adulation we associate more with our own celebrity culture than with the heyday of Victorian values. Dvořák's emotional life is equally enigmatic. He married the sister of his first love Josefina Čermáková, and was clearly a devoted family man; but most summers of his adult life were spent on the southern Bohemian estate where Josefina lived with her husband, and where much of Dvořák's finest music was written. Even his personal appearance seems curiously undefinitive. In photographs his eyes look out at us with precisely that disorientating mixture of truculence and vulnerability so often noted by his contemporaries.

Both his close friend Leoš Janáček and his son-in-law Josef Suk remarked on the fact that Dvořák seemed to think entirely in music. And it is of course in the music itself that these tensions and paradoxes are gloriously resolved. It is music in which the national traditions Dvořák inherited are fused with the Viennese Classical tradition of the masters he loved: Haydn, Mozart, Beethoven and Schubert. It is at once (and in the true sense of the words) popular and intellectual: Dvořák was genuinely a man of the people, and accessibility was a guiding principle for him, but he was also as severe a technical taskmaster where his own compositions were concerned as he was with those of his students. Perhaps above all, it is music of generous emotional range, capable of encompassing and sublimating, sometimes within a single work, the universal extremes of human feeling. What the great Dvořák scholar John Clapham wrote of that epitomic work the Piano Quintet, Op. 81 applies equally to all of Dvořák's most characteristic music: 'Laughter and tears, sorrow and gaiety, are found side by side, as well as many moods that lie between... All are presented with consummate mastery, they are decked in a wide range of instrumental colouring, and through the whole work sweeps the life-blood of vital rhythm.'

As this book will show, Dvořák's road to mastery was a long one, his path to recognition even longer. On both he met his share of reverses, and he developed in consequence a healthy scepticism towards popularity and the almost institutional status that grew from it. By his final years he was one of the best-known and best-loved composers of his time, his music performed and celebrated throughout the Old World and the New; but the only judgement on which he was prepared to rely remained that of his own artistic conscience, and his perspective was a long one. 'They like something today and jeer at it tomorrow,' he was once quoted as saying. '...So not even the greatest success causes me to become conceited. I work with integrity and do best in that way. This conviction gives me the greatest satisfaction. If I have created something for posterity, then my devotion to music and work of many years will have fulfilled its most splendid purpose.' It has, and millions of music lovers throughout the world continue to speak for posterity's gratitude.

Dvořák: His Life and Music

Chapter 1

The Butcher's Boy
(1841–1857)

This intrusion of modernity seems
to have instilled in the eight-year-old
Toník an enduring fascination with
all things locomotive...

The Butcher's Boy (1841–1857)

At the beginning of Dvořák's opera *The Jacobin* the curtain rises on a typical scene of Bohemian village life. On the left is an inn, on the right a church, from which emerges the sound of cheerful singing. A castle looms in the background. The story that will develop in this unpretentious setting represents a tribute to the living tradition of Bohemian music making and a glowing affirmation of the social and spiritual power of music itself. The stage directions might serve equally well for the opening scene of the composer's own life.

The village of Nelahozeves, where Antonín Dvořák was born on 8 September 1841, lies some 20 kilometres north of Prague, near the small town of Kralupy nad Vltavou. Clustered on the bank of the Vltava – the same river that runs through the Bohemian capital, and that Smetana would immortalise in his cycle of symphonic poems *Má vlast* – the village is dominated by the monolithic Renaissance castle of the Lobkowicz princes. The Lobkowiczes were one of the grandest noble families of the Austrian Empire, and could count among the beneficiaries of their musical patronage such figures as Beethoven and Gluck; more prosaically, they also employed as steward one Josef Zdeněk, the father of Dvořák's mother Anna. The composer's father, František, was a butcher and village innkeeper. Antonín, the eldest of the couple's eight surviving children, was born in the village inn and baptised

the following day in the church just across the road. (Dvořák was to remain a devout Catholic throughout his life, attending Mass regularly and typically ending his scores with the words 'Bohu díky', 'Thanks be to God'.) 'Leopold' was later added to his baptismal name, presumably at confirmation, but the boy was known to family and friends as Toník – a somehow less incongruous diminutive than the English equivalent, Tony.

Nelahozeves, showing the Lobkowicz castle, c. 1840, by W. Kandler

Despite his maternal grandfather's links with the Lobkowicz princes, both sides of the family were of peasant stock, and had been for generations. The composer was proud of his roots, and even at the height of his international fame he continued to feel most at ease with people from his own background among the rural labouring classes. To the end of his life he went out of his way to present himself as a simple Czech countryman, preferring drinks with his working-class neighbours to the formality of official receptions, and enjoying the music of the village band as heartily as the repertoire of the world's great orchestras.

3

Dvořák's birthplace
at Nelahozeves

František, whom a surviving photograph shows to have had the same broad Slavic face and unnerving stare as his famous son, had taken over the lease of the Nelahozeves butcher's shop from his father, and naturally expected Antonín to take it over from him in his turn. Indeed, there was little in Dvořák's immediate background to presage his remarkable talent. As a child of the village hostelry, he was no doubt exposed to the folk music traditions of his native land from the earliest age; but so were countless other peasant boys who never pursued a musical career, let alone aspired to the pantheon of great composers. Again, František was a dab hand at the zither, for which he composed the occasional dance number, and he may even have been a capable enough violinist to give his young son lessons. But music was part of the everyday life of communities like Nelahozeves, and such accomplishments were nothing out of the ordinary. Whatever the sources of

Dvořák's gifts, however, they clearly showed themselves early. The childhood of great artists is fertile territory for hindsight, and the story that Toník was already entertaining the pub's customers on the fiddle by the time he was five is almost certainly apocryphal; but there seems no reason to doubt that even during the years of his primary education music was his principal interest.

He probably started at the village school in early October 1847. The curriculum was limited, but for a child of humble origins with a natural flair for music there could hardly have been a more fruitful environment in mid-nineteenth-century Europe than a Bohemian village school. As the English musicologist Charles Burney famously noted on his tour through the area in 1772, music was as central to the syllabus as the three Rs, and it was typical for the local schoolmaster also to be the church organist and choirmaster, a combination of roles encompassed by the term Kantor. So it was with Josef Spitz at Nelahozeves, who appears to have been an especially lovable specimen of the breed. A central figure in the village and the first working musician to take Dvořák under his wing, Spitz began the long process of providing his young charge with a practical (if not yet formal) underpinning to his innate talent. He seems to have been responsible for giving Toník his earliest piano lessons and for involving him in the vibrant musical life of Nelahozeves and the surrounding area.

In an interview he gave to the *Sunday Times* in 1885 Dvořák could still recall with affection the merrymaking after Sunday evening Mass in Nelahozeves:

> *On Sunday, when church is over, they begin their music and dancing, and often keep it up without cessation till early in the following morning. Each village has its band of eight or ten musicians – I belonged to ours as soon as I could fiddle a*

little. It is supported by the dancers, who pay nothing to go in, but in the middle of their polka or waltz a couple is stopped by one of the musicians and not allowed to continue until they have paid as many kreutzers as they can afford. When all is over, the band divide their earnings, and mine, of course, used to be handed forthwith to my father.

He also left an account of his first nervous steps as solo performer outside the smoky comfort of the inn. Remembering many years later how he had given himself a good talking to before his debut as a violinist in the village church, he told Václav Novotný, the Czech journalist and critic who accompanied him on one of his trips to England:

...what a fuss I was in at that time and how afraid I was when I tuned my fiddle and how my bow shook at the first notes. But it turned out all right. When I had finished, there was a hum and buzz throughout the whole choir, everybody pressed round me – my friends smiled happily at me and clapped me good-naturedly on the shoulder, and our neighbour, the leader of the violins, gave me a whole groschen.

The young Toník seems also to have performed at Veltrusy, with its exquisite Baroque chateau and 'English' park, and at Vepřek, the home of his father's older brother Josef. He was another innkeeper and amateur musician whose local reputation as violinist and trumpeter no doubt looms larger in retrospect than it might have done had his nephew followed him into the meat and drink trade.

Apart from anecdotes told by the composer or remembered by family and friends, little is known about the course of Dvořák's schooling at Nelahozeves. There were, however, two developments in the wider world during his schooldays which were to have a direct influence on Dvořák's future interests. One, incongruously enough, was the construction of a railway line from Prague to Kralupy. The track ran through Nelahozeves and was opened in June 1850, the Archduke Albrecht himself processing along it in a special train. This intrusion of modernity seems to have instilled in the eight-year-old Toník an enduring fascination with all things locomotive: even when he had established himself as one of the world's most celebrated composers he would visit the nearest railway station as often as he could to note down engine numbers and to talk technicalities with the drivers. He once declared that he would have given all his symphonies to have invented the steam train. The construction of the line also brought an influx of immigrant workers to the village, and with them new folksongs, such as those of the Italian tunnel-blasters who drank and sang at František's inn at the end of their day's labours.

The second development, more portentously, was the wave of revolutions which swept across Europe in 1848 and which included a brief and abortive Czech nationalist insurrection in June. The immediate effect of the risings was an Act of Emancipation which promised greater civil liberties for the subjects of the Austrian Empire (including a relaxation of the curbs on national languages such as Czech), but such liberalisation was swiftly reversed under the new emperor, the eighteen-year-old Franz Josef, whose long reign would last until twelve years after Dvořák's death. As a result, while Czech was the language of everyday life in the Bohemian countryside, German remained the language of authority: to its Habsburg overlords, Nelahozeves was known as Mühlhausen, and the Vltava as the Moldau. German was therefore also the language of advancement, as crucial to a young man's prospects in the mid-nineteenth century as it had been in the Czech lands since the Habsburgs' defeat of the Czech nobility at the Battle of the White Mountain in 1620. It was natural, then, that when Dvořák left the village school in the summer of 1853 his parents would want him, whatever further training they expected him to undertake, to acquire a working knowledge of German. With this in mind, they packed him off, shortly after his twelfth birthday, to the nearby small town of Zlonice (Zlonitz), where he lived for the next two years.

Until recently it was generally believed that the young Toník was sent to Zlonice principally to improve his knowledge of the butchering business. Indeed, the idea that Dvořák was destined for the life of a butcher and had to fight tooth and nail to change his father's mind has proved remarkably persistent. In fact, there is no evidence whatsoever that Toník went to Zlonice to pursue a butchering apprenticeship or that he undertook any such training while he was there. Bizarrely enough, the certificate of apprenticeship dated November 1856, and long cited as proof of František's continuing obduracy in the matter of his son's career, is now recognised as a later forgery. (The conjunction of two romantic archetypes – the rags-to-riches story and the youthful struggle against an uncomprehending world – clearly exerts a potent hold on the imagination of biographers. That Dvořák himself was cannily alert to the myth-making potential of his early years is evident from his asking a friend to exploit the Czech publicity value of an 1886 *Pall Mall Gazette* interview because 'The article is under the title "From Butcher to Baton", thus very catchy.') A career as butcher–innkeeper had probably not yet been ruled out, but there is certainly no indication that his family were pressuring him to pursue it. He went to Zlonice to complete his general education, with particular emphasis on improving his German and developing his musical knowledge.

Zlonice, at the heart of a coal-mining area, was an altogether more cosmopolitan place than Nelahozeves. It was also the home of Dvořák's maternal uncle, Antonín Zdeněk. A steward to the local landowner, Count Kinský, Zdeněk and his wife had recently lost their only son and were no doubt happy to have their nephew's company as a lodger. The town not only provided a better general education than was open to him at home, it also offered a far richer array of musical opportunities. The headmaster of the local school, Josef Toman, was also, almost by definition, the church organist and choirmaster, as well as a violinist, trumpeter and double bass player; and the German teacher Antonín Liehmann was to prove perhaps the most significant influence on the course of Dvořák's future life.

Liehmann was Spitz writ large. A somewhat volatile individual in his mid-forties, he was a teacher by profession but a musician by vocation. He played the organ, violin, clarinet and horn, directed his own private chamber orchestra and was an experienced composer whose works were locally much in demand. (It was in one of these that Dvořák had made his jittery debut in the church at Nelahozeves.) In addition to coaching him in German, Liehmann taught Antonín the viola, organ and piano, and the fundamentals of harmony. His abrasive teaching style belonged more to the eighteenth century than to the nineteenth: 'Liehmann was a good musician,' Dvořák told his own pupil Josef Michl in later years, 'but he was quick tempered and still taught according to the old methods: if a pupil could not play a passage, he got as many cuffs as there were notes on the sheet.' But Dvořák recognised the debt he owed to this hard schooling, and he remained grateful for it to the end of his life.

As a member of Liehmann's private band, Antonín gained access to the houses of the local nobility, including his uncle's employer Count Kinský, who was one of Liehmann's patrons. Dvořák's first surviving composition dates from this period, the modest 'Forget-me-not' Polka for piano (B.1), which frames a trio section by Liehmann himself. One of Dvořák's favourite anecdotes concerned another polka apparently written around the same time. As he told the *Sunday Times* thirty years later:

> *Once, I recollect, I determined to try my hand at a score myself. I wrote a polka for strings, 2 clarinets, 1 cornet, 2 horns, and 1 trombone. With great pride I carried it home to Mühlhausen and had it tried by our band there. How anxiously I waited for the opening chord! It was all right, bar the cornet part, which I had got quite in the wrong key. The mistake was soon remedied by transposition, but I leave you to guess the effect.*

Dvořák finished at the Zlonice school in the summer of 1855. At around the same time he was joined by the rest of his family, František having decided to relocate to Zlonice's Big Inn in the hope of richer pickings than Nelahozeves was offering. (František soon crossed swords with entrenched local interests and blotted his copybook with the police by serving drinks after hours. Within four years he had moved his family on to the industrial town of Kladno, to the west of Prague, where success in business continued to elude him. In later years he turned to his zither to make ends meet, while Dvořák provided discreet financial support.) At whatever stage the scales tilted in favour of a musical career, Toník does seem to have helped out in the family shop during the year after he left the Zlonice school, and it is almost certainly to this period that his recorded memories of the butchering life belong, including the famous anecdote of his being dragged through the mud by a runaway heifer while bringing it home from market in nearby Velvary. If by 1855 František needed any further convincing about his son's true vocation, however, there were persuasive local advocates whom Toník could marshal to his cause – notably Liehmann, who was quick to see his pupil's exceptional promise, but also, and conclusively once he threw his funds behind a musical training, Uncle Antonín himself. Most likely, though, his parents were happy enough to encourage his musical ambitions. Certainly, when in the autumn of 1856 Dvořák moved to the north Bohemian town of Česká Kamenice (Böhmisch-Kamnitz) to continue his studies in German, everyone concerned seems to have accepted that it was not because it would help him expand the family business, but because it was the official language of the Prague music schools.

Česká Kamenice lay in the German-speaking region of Bohemia which would find itself in the international spotlight eighty years later as the Sudetenland of Hitler's territorial ambitions. Dvořák moved there on an exchange basis with a local miller's son and enrolled in the municipal school for a year. A fellow-student remembered the fifteen-year-old new boy as lively, witty and immensely sociable, a description strikingly at odds with Dvořák's later image but perhaps indicative of a youth feeling confident for the first time in his sense of professional direction.

The Česká Kamenice school, too, had its resident Kantor – one František Hancke – who proved a worthy successor to Spitz and Lichmann in bringing to Dvořák's musical education the benefit of his own formal training at the Prague Organ School. Dvořák also seems to have made progress with his German (though in later life he tended to downplay his proficiency in it), and when in the summer of 1857 he returned to Zlonice he brought with him not only valuable experience in organ-playing and choir conducting but also a certificate of distinction in the core subjects of the Česká Kamenice curriculum. A few weeks later, shortly after his sixteenth birthday in September 1857, father and son loaded a handcart with Antonín's scanty possessions and set out to walk the thirty-five kilometres to Prague, the city that was to be Dvořák's principal home for the rest of his life.

Chapter 2

The Years of Apprenticeship (1857–1872)

When he used to write at the table, he held the quill in his teeth and played with his fingers on his jacket or on his legs.

The Years of Apprenticeship (1857–1872)

With his arrival in the Bohemian capital Dvořák's real apprenticeship began. Mid-nineteenth-century Prague was a provincial outpost of the Austrian Empire, its political life as completely dominated by Vienna as was the landscape of Dvořák's childhood by the Lobkowicz castle. Memories of the barricades were still green – the Czech rising had been brutally suppressed here only nine years before Dvořák first set foot in the cobbled streets – but equally strong was Prague's pride in its musical heritage, not least as the city that had taken Mozart to its heart when his star was waning in Vienna. Prague boasted two schools of music, the Conservatoire and the Organ School, and it was at the latter that Dvořák enrolled in the autumn of 1857. As at Zlonice, he lodged with relatives, moving in first with his cousin Marie Plívová and her husband Jan Plíva, a master tailor, and then with his aunt Josefa (his father's sister) and her husband Václav Dušek, who worked for the railway and with whom we can assume Dvořák deepened his knowledge of locomotives. By then, however, he was already a year into his musical studies.

Founded in 1830, the Institute for the Training of Organists and Choir Directors of the Association for the Cultivation of Church Music, to give it its full title, provided a solid if conservative training in composition and organ technique. Its teachers included Karel Pitsch, the principal when Dvořák began his studies, and Josef Krejčí, who took over when Pitsch died in 1858 and who went on to become Director of the Conservatoire. Based in arcaded buildings in Konviktská (Konviktgasse), the school had a first-rate reputation. In addition to Dvořák himself, its distinguished alumni would include the composers Leoš Janáček, Karel Bendl and Josef Bohuslav Foerster, whose father taught there during Dvořák's time.

Like most areas of official life in Prague, classes at the Organ School were conducted in German, and during his first year Dvořák continued to take German lessons at the school of the Franciscan monastery of Maria Schnee (Our Lady of the Snows). He later claimed that his time at the Organ School was blighted by his stumbling German, but since the Maria Schnee school officially rated it as exemplary it is hard to know how compromised by later motives his memories may have been. (He also claimed, for example, that he was mocked for composing – hardly an eccentric activity for a music student.) Whatever his difficulties in class, however, he received a firm foundation in harmony, counterpoint and fugue at the Organ School, as well as a sound training in practical musicianship. He was also introduced to the work of the Baroque and Classical masters who were to be an abiding influence on his own work, including Bach, Handel, Mozart, Beethoven and Schubert.

Just as important, the school gave Dvořák a base from which to explore the abundant musical life of the capital, even if his ability to take advantage of it was severely hindered by lack of funds. Within weeks of commencing his studies he had joined the viola section of one of Prague's flourishing concert-giving organisations, the St Cecilia Society, whose conductor, Antonín Apt, had a passion for Wagner, the *bête noire* of the

Organ School authorities. The society's concerts gave Dvořák his first intoxicating taste of the 'new German music'. They also gave him a foothold in the overlapping circles of Prague's practising musicians, and from time to time he probably found himself drafted into other orchestras, including that of the Estates Theatre. He cultivated the friendship of other musicians, including his fellow student Karel Bendl, who not only lent his colleague scores but also allowed him to use his piano for want of one at Dvořák's own lodgings; it was to Bendl's generosity and expertise, he later said, that he owed his knowledge of Beethoven's symphonies. Through the St Cecilia orchestra Dvořák also met Adolf Čech, who was to become an influential promoter of his work on the concert platform, and whose pen portrait of his fellow viola player already suggests some sort of transformation from the bright, outgoing adolescent of Česká Kamenice days:

'You will play at the same desk as Dvořák,' said Apt, and introduced me to a young man with a mane of typically tousled, thick black hair... So I began to play with Dvořák, but I can tell you it was no easy matter. Now my playing did not please him, now he was annoyed with the next desk, another time he was dissatisfied with the conductor – or with himself. And now and again he would stop playing and start humming some scrap of melody to himself.

It was often through friends, too, that he managed to sneak into rehearsals, or into concerts for which he could never have afforded a ticket. In March 1858 he heard Liszt conduct his own works in Prague, and a year later attended concerts given by Hans von Bülow (later one of his strongest advocates) and the recently widowed Clara Schumann. He may also have heard Weber's *Der Freischütz* at the Estates Theatre. But the performance which most stuck in his mind was of Beethoven's 'Choral' Symphony: he slipped into Spohr's rehearsals of the work during the Conservatoire's golden jubilee celebrations in July 1858, and nearly thirty years later could still recall the occasion with undiminished excitement as the 'first real orchestral performance I ever heard'. For all such moments of revelation, however, his poverty must often have made Prague's concert life seem like a feast of Tantalus.

Dvořák graduated from the Organ School in July 1859, with the second highest place in the final examinations. (Sigmund Glanz, who won the top prize, is lost to musical history.) The examiners' report stressed his practical skill, and they no doubt expected him to take up a secure position as organist at one of the city's churches. Surprisingly, given his credentials, Dvořák's application for the post of organist at the church of St Henry (Svaty Jindřich) was turned down. But his heart seems not to have been in it. Within weeks of his graduation he had joined a dance band as viola player, and he simply stayed on with them instead, playing polkas and medleys at restaurants and balls around the city, with occasional forays into the 'legitimate' repertoire at the concert hall romantically situated on Žofin Island in the Vltava. The bandleader, Karel Komzák – himself an organist (Dvořák sometimes stood in for him at the organ of the local lunatic asylum) – ran a tight ship, and his little orchestra was doing very well for itself on the dance circuit. It was the beginning of a hand-to-mouth freelance existence that would provide Dvořák with a precarious income for years to come. For an aspiring composer, however, it was all grist to the creative mill. What's more, within three years Dvořak's membership of Komzák's band would give him a front seat at that remarkable Czech cultural renaissance of the 1860s which found its greatest institutional expression in the new National

Theatre and of which Dvořák himself would in time become the international face.

For twelve years Dvořák made his living as a viola player, supplementing his income by teaching. It is a period of biographical shadow and creative ferment. To his colleagues his outward life must have seemed uneventful, unenviable even. He was still staying mainly with relatives, despite a brief and none too successful experiment in communal living (with, among others, Mořic Anger – in later years a tireless exponent of Dvořák's music). Earning a pittance, he was apparently failing to capitalise on the auspicious start that his Organ School training had given him. Certainly by the standards of most composers of the first rank his apprenticeship was long indeed. Mozart and Schubert were his idols; but by the age at which Dvořák achieved his first popular success Schubert was already dead, and if it had taken Mozart as long to reach maturity as a composer we would be lamenting a promise cut off just as it was starting to be fulfilled.

But behind the routine of earning his keep lay another routine, and one of which only his closest associates were aware. Throughout this time he was composing prolifically (chamber music, symphonies, songs, even operas), experimenting with forms and forces, learning his chosen craft with a pen between his teeth and a keyboard under his fingers. Impatient though his ambition must sometimes have made him, he was also exercising the severest self-criticism. He destroyed much of his early output – in later life he said he had never been short of paper for a fire during these years – and we are reliant on his far from infallible memory for a full account of the compositions he completed. What remains, immature though much of it is, offers a picture of a composer painstakingly working his way towards a personal voice, and a tantalising glimpse of an œuvre perhaps substantially lost to posterity.

Dvořák's first surviving chamber work, and the first composition to which he gave an opus number, dates from the second half of 1861, a couple of years after he joined Komzák's band: the three-movement String Quintet in A minor (B.7). A gift for melody is evident in the central slow movement, with its opulent viola tune, but there is little else, even with the benefit of hindsight, to mark it out as the work of Dvořák; indeed, the opening motif of the finale is so like that of the first movement of Mozart's Piano Quartet in G minor (K.478) as surely to be a case of unconscious recall. Dvořák revisited the manuscript in later years, but it was not performed until 1921, long after the composer's death, and was published only in 1943.

The second surviving composition to which Dvořák gave an opus number is also a chamber work: the String Quartet in A major (B.8), dating from March 1862. It is dedicated to his old teacher at the Organ School, Josef Krejčí, and has a Schubertian freshness, especially in the first of its four thematically linked movements. Despite such felicities as the haunting main subject of the slow movement, the quartet is typical of much of Dvořák's early work in being overlong for its ideas, even after the substantial cuts he made while revising it for its first performance in 1888. As his willingness to keep it in the repertoire suggests, however, it remains an engaging work, an attractive forerunner for the thirteen string quartets that were to follow.

Whatever Dvořák may have written over the next three years, none of it survived his private bonfires of the vanities. As he later put it, speaking of this period of his creative life, it was 'not that I was unable to produce music, but I had not technique enough to express all that was in me. I had ideas but I could not utter them perfectly'. Perhaps the pace of change around him left less time for composition anyway, because in the early 1860s the currents of musical life in Prague were drawing him inexorably towards the very centre of what has become known as the Czech revival.

Ever since the defeat of the Habsburg forces by Napoleon III at the battles of Magenta and Solferino in 1859, the spirit of Czech nationalism – crushed but not extinguished a decade earlier – had begun to stir again. In Prague it manifested itself in the concerted campaign of the conservative Old Czech (staročeši) and radical Young Czech (mladočeši) parties for a theatre dedicated to the production of operas and plays in Czech – a dream of nationalists since at least 1844. The decisive first stage of this National Theatre project came to fruition amid great popular rejoicing in November 1862, albeit in cramped temporary accommodation rather

The Provisional Theatre, Prague

limply dubbed the Provisional Theatre (Prozatímní divadlo). (It would be another six years before the foundation stone of a permanent theatre was laid.) The conductorship of the new theatre went not to Smetana, who had returned from self-imposed exile in Sweden in the hope of obtaining it, but to the relatively unknown Jan Nepomuk Maýr, and it is a tribute to Komzák's standards and connections that his band was conscripted to form the core of the Provisional Theatre's orchestra. For Dvořák, this development marked a turning point in his professional life. From being simply an obscure player in a touring dance band, he had become at a stroke the principal viola of the most prestigious Czech cultural enterprise of the century.

The change gave Dvořák access to swathes of the operatic repertoire previously closed to him, including the works of Rossini, Donizetti, Verdi, Meyerbeer, Gluck and Glinka. It took some time for Czech composers to catch up with the ambitions of the theatre's founding fathers, but when they did so Dvořák also played in the groundbreaking Czech operas of Smetana – *The Brandenburgers in Bohemia*, *The Bartered Bride* and *Dalibor* – whose subjects and procedures were to leave their mark on his own operatic work.

Until Komzák's band was formally subsumed into the Provisional Theatre orchestra in 1865, Dvořák must have led a musically schizophrenic life, playing café waltzes one day and grand opera the next, as well as appearing at concerts organised by such bodies as the Academic Reading Union and the newly founded Artistic Society (Umělecká beseda). In retrospect, though, this period can perhaps be seen as the crucible for that seemingly effortless fusion of the popular and the learned so characteristic of his music and so central to its enduring appeal in the concert halls of Europe and the New World from the final quarter of the nineteenth century.

It was at three concerts held on Žofín Island in February
and November 1863 that Dvořák played under the baton of
Richard Wagner, whose music – the embodiment of German
modernism – exerted the same kind of spell over forward-
looking musicians of Dvořák's generation as Schoenberg's
would exert over musicians of Pierre Boulez's generation
in Paris a century later. Dvořák acknowledged that the
excitement of playing some of Wagner's latest compositions
under the composer's own direction spilled over into a hero
worship bordering on stalking. 'I was perfectly crazy about
him,' he told an interviewer on a visit to England more than

twenty years later, 'and recollect following him as he walked along the streets to get a chance now and again of seeing the great little man's face.' Among the works he played under Wagner in 1863 were the preludes to *Die Meistersinger* and *Tristan und Isolde*, and the overture to *Tannhäuser*, echoes of which were to surface in his music for years to come. Indeed, it can be argued that the assimilation of Wagner's overpowering influence was the greatest challenge Dvořák faced in his struggle to develop an individual musical voice.

The year 1865 was a pivotal one in Dvořák's life. Even by his exalted later standards, it was extraordinarily productive. During the course of it he wrote not only two full-length symphonies, but also a cello concerto (which remained in short score) and a song cycle, as well as a couple of songs for baritone and piano. Hazardous though it is to make direct connections between the work and personal circumstances of an artist of his standing, it is hard not to see in this remarkable outpouring of music a reflection of what we know of Dvořák's emotional life at the time.

His Dušek cousin Anna, with whose parents he was once again living during this period, left an affectionate, if somewhat idealised, portrait of the composer as family lodger:

> *He had a piano hired from his tailor at 2 gulden a month, a table opposite it, and behind [it] his bed. He often composed immediately on waking – in bed, and whenever he got an idea, he played it over on the eiderdown. When he used to write at the table, he held the quill in his teeth and played with his fingers on his jacket or on his legs. After a while he went to the piano and played it over, singing softly at the same time... I never heard my cousin speak vulgarly, flippantly or indelicately. He was through and through of noble character, of high morals, and his conduct was without reproach. He*

The Čermáková sisters, Josefina (standing) and Anna

*never came home late, he had no female acquaintances and
no love affairs, and in our family they used to say that 'Anton
was afraid of women'. I remember him saying on occasion:
'That's a pretty girl!' but that was as far as he went.*

If this is an accurate picture, then, at least in the last respect, Dvořák's secrecy was not confined to composing. Among his new piano pupils in 1865 were two daughters of a Prague goldsmith, Josefina and Anna Čermáková. Josefina was an attractive young woman of sixteen, already making a name for herself as an actress, and Dvořák seems to have fallen deeply in love with her. A photograph from exactly this time shows the twenty-four-year-old Dvořák as a striking young man with a dark moustache and somewhat searching gaze, an image far from the familiar picture of the middle-aged composer with his wild beard, bulbous nose and receding hairline. But whatever his personal attractions, Josefina was having none of this penniless jobbing musician, and rejected his advances. (Like Haydn and Mozart before him, Dvořák later transferred his affections to the younger sister, who would become his wife; but at this stage Anna was just eleven years old.)

The song cycle *Cypresses* ('Cypřiše') (B.11) is surely a musical embodiment of these joys and trials. A setting of eighteen romantic lyrics, conventional expressions of love and longing by the poet Gustav Pfleger-Moravský, the cycle was written in just over a fortnight in July 1865. The musical voice is less than assured, and critics have pointed to Dvořák's errors in declamation: Czech words are always stressed on the first syllable, a prosodic inflexibility not naturally suited to the established idioms of Romantic song. *Cypresses* therefore offers the unusual spectacle of a composer having to learn how to set his own language. (Smetana, whose natural first language was German, was also still wrestling with the

Dvořák, aged about twenty-four

challenge of Czech prosody.) It seems unlikely, however, that Dvořák's almost compulsive revisiting of the cycle in later life was purely a matter of refining his word setting. Songs from the cycle feature in his operas, and in the early 1880s he revised six of them for two miniature song cycles (B.123 & 124). One of the six was also among the eight songs from *Cypresses* which he revised as *Love Songs* ('Písně milostné') (B.160) in 1888. A year earlier he had made arrangements of twelve of the songs for string quartet (B.152) under the title *Echo of Songs* ('Ohlas písní'), and motifs from one of the songs appear in *Silhouettes* (B.32) for piano, written during the 1870s; this set of miniatures also re-marshals themes from the other major works of 1865, Dvořák's first two symphonies. Echoes, silhouettes: it is as if he needed unconsciously to keep returning to the music of that year in order to process the events themselves.

Cypresses may have had the strongest emotional resonance for the composer himself, but of greater significance for his future musical development are the two symphonies. Long regarded as apprentice works, they are certainly typical of much of his earliest surviving output in showing greater fertility of ideas than discipline in regulating them. Nonetheless, the Symphony No. 1 (B.9), nicknamed by the composer himself, more for nostalgic than musical reasons, 'The Bells of Zlonice' ('Zlonické zvony'), is remarkable in several ways, not the least of which is that Dvořák turned to the symphonic form at all. There were, after all, few home-grown models for him to draw on: Smetana wrote only one symphony, the decidedly un-Czech *Triumf-Symphonie* of 1854, which for political reasons makes great play of Haydn's 'Emperor's Hymn'; while the otherwise precocious Zdeněk Fibich only published his first symphony in 1883. Among non-Czechs, Bruckner, seventeen years Dvořák's senior, was yet to complete his first symphony, as was Dvořák's near-contemporary Tchaikovsky; while Brahms, as daunted as he was inspired by Beethoven's example, delayed finishing his first until 1876 (by which time Dvořák had five under his belt). Nor was the symphony any longer the inevitable form to choose for a composer of Dvořák's generation and aesthetic leanings. But choose it he did, and the results are striking. Beethovenian in ambition – it shares both its overall key (C minor) and the keys of its four movements with Beethoven's Fifth – Dvořák's Symphony No. 1 is notable for the self-confidence with which it takes on its Classical forebears. The composer thought well enough of it at the time to submit it for a German musical competition, but it probably escaped the flames only because the judges failed to return the manuscript; in later years he mistakenly recalled destroying it. The symphony resurfaced in 1923 in the possession of (an unrelated) Dr Rudolf Dvořák, who had bought it from a secondhand bookseller, and it was another thirteen years before it was performed.

When asked by a student how he felt about the supposed disappearance of his symphony, Dvořák replied that he had simply sat down and written another one. This, the Symphony No. 2 in B flat major (B.12), was composed in ten weeks and finished less than seven months after the first. It is a more ambitious and arguably less coherent work, with the influence of Wagner beginning to make itself felt, particularly in the outer movements. Indeed, perhaps the most telling evidence of immaturity lies in the striking difference in idiom between the two symphonies, despite their having been written so close together. Dvořák revised the Second Symphony in 1887 for performance the following year, and this is the form in which it makes occasional appearances in the repertoire today.

Dvořák was later to describe the years between 1866 and 1871 as his 'mad period'. On the surface his everyday life continued much as before. His daily bread still came from his work as viola player with the Provisional Theatre orchestra (the Komzák band no longer existed outside it) and from his private teaching. There were changes at the theatre – Smetana came into his rightful inheritance as conductor in 1866, and Czech operas were beginning to appear among the Czech translations of Rossini, Gounod and Verdi – but they affected Dvořák only insofar as they enabled him to expand his knowledge of the repertoire. However, in his creative life, still hidden from all but his most intimate circle, it was a period of restless experimentation.

One can only wonder at the single-mindedness with which he continued to follow the demands of his craft and at the self-discipline with which, as his twenties advanced, he consistently placed authenticity of work above the lure of recognition. Indeed, he later destroyed a great deal of what he had written during this period, and much of what remains survives only by chance. From 1866 to 1869, for example, we have only a single work, the *Intermezzi* (or *Interludes*) for small orchestra (B.15) – seven short pieces with the smell of greasepaint about them, a flexing, perhaps, of his own theatrical ambitions as he watched those new Czech operas from his desk in the orchestra pit.

Three string quartets, all apparently completed during 1870, have come down to us only because copies of the parts survived after Dvořák destroyed the original scores. Presumably his first since the quartet of 1862, these works demonstrate just how searching was his pursuit of technical mastery during the intervening years. Gone are the high Classical forms of his first two chamber compositions. Instead, all three works are to a greater or lesser extent essays in the formal principles of Liszt and Wagner applied to the medium of the quartet. The String Quartet No. 2 in B flat major (B.17) was probably the first to be written. The first three of its four movements are monothematic; even the scherzo is trio-less. The deeply felt opening pages of the finale, which have something of the atmosphere of the 'Heiliger Dankgesang' from Beethoven's late Quartet in A minor, Op. 132, introduce a heterogeneous movement which incorporates material from the first movement (as well as an enigmatic allusion to the 'Wedding March' from Mendelssohn's incidental music to *A Midsummer Night's Dream*).

The String Quartet No. 3 in D major (B.18) takes to a new extreme Dvořák's early tendency to prolixity, its four movements running to well over an hour of music – an expansiveness of treatment which its ideas are scarcely distinguished enough to support. The scherzo contains a vivid reminder of the political turbulence of the decade in its use of the banned Slavonic folksong *Hej, Slované!* – a nationalist rallying cry of the late 1860s, which in its Polish form was to become that country's national anthem.

The third of the set, the String Quartet No. 4 in E minor (B.19), is the most experimental of all, being conceived, highly unusually for a quartet of this period, as a single continuous movement with contrasting sections. The overheated musical language of the fast sections is the least Dvořákian yet, but the meditative central section, marked *Andante religioso*, would have several later incarnations: first as a slow movement in his String Quintet in G major (B.49) of 1875; then, when he could not make it fit there either, as a stand-alone work for string orchestra, the *Nocturne* in B major (B.47), published in 1883 as Opus 40; he also produced versions for violin and piano (B.48a) and piano duet (B.48b).

The existence of parts for these quartets suggests that Dvořák played them through with friends before deciding they did not pass muster. No such possibility was open to him for another work on which he was engaged at the same time. This was his most ambitious project yet, nothing less than a three-act heroic opera. Dvořák himself adapted the libretto from an early-nineteenth-century play by the Romantic poet Karl Theodor Körner about, of all subjects, King Alfred. The whole thing was an extraordinary undertaking for an unknown composer, and Dvořák took care to keep it even more than usually secret. It is unsurprising that the work was conceived on Wagnerian lines. That the text is in German, on the other hand, is so surprising as to be almost incomprehensible, both because the Provisional Theatre would only stage works in Czech and because Dvořák could have chosen so recondite a story only because he saw in the Saxons' struggle against the Danes an allegory of the Czechs' struggle for independence from Austrian hegemony. (To compound the ironies, the opera itself was first performed in Olomouc in December 1938, less than three months after the Sudetenland was ceded to Hitler under the Munich Agreement.) Completed in October 1870, *Alfred* (B.16) went straight into the bottom drawer. Dvořák never let on that he had written it, but he obviously could not bring himself to destroy it either. Some years later he dug out the overture as a concert piece under the title *Tragic Overture*, which in turn became the *Dramatic Overture* (B.16a) when it was published after his death.

1871 was a watershed year for Dvořák. In June he finally went public as a composer, letting it be known through the pages of the Prague music journal *Hudební listy* that he was working on an opera. (As with his symphonies, when his first attempt at opera proved fruitless he had simply started again.) The following month he took the decisive step of resigning from his post in the Provisional Theatre orchestra after nine years as principal viola, cutting himself adrift from his only secure source of income.

Why did he choose this particular moment to cross the professional Rubicon? Perhaps his work at the Provisional Theatre was leaving him too little time for composition, which he had clearly seen for years as the main purpose of his life. Perhaps, with his thirtieth birthday fast approaching, he simply felt it was now or never. Certainly he had found an influential supporter in the editor of *Hudební listy*, the well-connected Prague lawyer and former pupil of Smetana, Dr Ludevít Procházka. Dvořák had shown him parts of his new opera and perhaps other pieces, and Procházka quickly followed up his first article about the new composer on the block with another praising his work. He also made space for Dvořák's compositions at the musical soirées that he and his wife held on the Prague drawing-room circuit – the first time that Dvořák's music had been heard in anything like a public forum. Works performed at these evenings included Dvořák's settings of five poems by Smetana's best-known librettist Eliška Krásnohorská (B.23), the ballad *The Orphan* ('Sirotek') (B.24) and part of a lost piano trio.

By the end of the year Dvořák had finished his new opera, his first as far as the outside world was concerned. This was an adaptation by an amateur librettist – a lawyer called Bernard Guldener – of an old puppet play, and it rejoiced in the less than compelling title of *Feel at Home, Mr Matthew* ('Pane Matěj, jako doma'). Set in early-seventeenth-century Bohemia, it is a story of mistaken identity and lovers' misunderstanding. The Matěj of the title, a charcoal burner, gives shelter to a stranger who loses himself in the forest and who turns out to be a king. Dvořák wisely rechristened it *King and Charcoal Burner* ('Král a uhlíř') (B.21), providing it with a Wagnerian score which he submitted to Smetana for consideration as a Provisional Theatre production. The response was positive, and Dvořák had every reason to think that his second foray into opera would soon appear on the stage. In April 1872 Smetana himself conducted the overture at a concert on Žofin Island, an occasion that marked a significant step-change in the size of Dvořák's audience. In November of the same year Procházka arranged for Dvořák's latest chamber work, the three-movement Piano Quintet in A major, Op. 5 (B.28), to be performed at a matinée concert at the Konvikt Hall by a star line-up of instrumentalists. The quintet marks a staging post on the composer's journey away from Wagner and towards a deeper assimilation of the Viennese Classical models of his earliest chamber music, but Dvořák remained unhappy with the score and later claimed to have destroyed it. Procházka kept a copy, though, from which Dvořák revised the work in 1887; the exercise prompted him to compose the famous Piano Quintet in A major, Op. 81 (B.155), which has overshadowed the earlier quintet ever since.

By the time the early quintet received its premiere there were ominous signs that *King and Charcoal Burner* was getting bogged down at the Provisional Theatre. But otherwise, as 1872 drew to a close, Dvořák could have been forgiven for congratulating himself on the way things were going. Two years earlier the musical public of Prague thought of him, if at all, as a viola player. His own music, laboured over between piano lessons and performances in cafés, ballrooms and theatres, was known only to his immediate circle, its true extent unsuspected even by them. Now at last he was starting to make a name for himself as a composer. He had influential sponsors promoting his interests, and his music was becoming heard in the salons and concert halls of his adopted city. His decision to take his chances as a freelance composer was starting to look like the right one. After years of obscurity and thankless dedication to his calling, the tide was finally turning in his favour.

Chapter 3

Breakthrough
(1873–1877)

It was probably after finishing *The Cunning Peasant* that Dvořák treated himself to one of his rare vacations: a walking holiday with an intense young Moravian musician he had got to know in Prague.

Breakthrough (1873–1877)

On 3 June 1872 Dvořák completed a score that would begin the real turnaround in his personal and professional prospects. The patriotic cantata *Hymn: The Heirs of the White Mountain* ('Hymnus: Dědicové bílé hory'), Op. 30 (B.27) is a stirring invocation of the spirit of Czech nationalism. The Battle of the White Mountain in 1620, at which the insurgent forces of the Protestant Bohemian nobility were defeated outside Prague by the armies of the Catholic Habsburgs, occupied a similar place in the Czech collective memory to that held by the Battle of Kosovo or the Battle of the Boyne for Serbian or Irish nationalists. The *Hymnus*, as it is generally known, is a setting of a poem by Vítězslav Hálek, one of the leading lights of nineteenth-century Czech letters. In the charged political atmosphere of 1870s Prague it was a shrewd choice. On 9 March 1873 the *Hymnus* was premiered by the Prague Hlalol Choral Society under the baton of the society's co-founder, Dvořák's old friend Karel Bendl. It was a triumph. The music – and perhaps still more the work's nationalist sentiments – struck a resounding chord with the audience, and the following morning Dvořák woke, like Byron after the publication of *Childe Harold*, to find himself famous. It was a circumscribed fame, no doubt – four years were still to pass before his gifts began to attract serious notice outside Prague – but for a man who until recently had been unknown even in the city that had been his home for a decade and a half, it was success indeed.

The popular and critical acclaim showered on the *Hymnus* – now ironically among Dvořák's least-performed works – seems to have broken whatever logjam was holding up *King and Charcoal Burner* at the Provisional Theatre, and Smetana put the opera into rehearsal in August. This further boost to Dvořák's professional hopes was to prove short-lived. Within a month it was clear that the singers and orchestra were struggling with the complex demands of the score, and in September it was withdrawn from the programme, Smetana commenting: 'It is a serious work, full of ideas and genius, but I don't believe it can be performed'. Dvořák's feelings can only be imagined, but his resilience was, as ever, extraordinary. In an exercise probably unique in musical history, the following year he took the libretto out again and reset the entire text to completely different music.

It may have been this rejection of the first version of *King and Charcoal Burner* that prompted Dvořák to cull his pre-1871 compositions. (He was still destroying new works that failed to measure up to his own standards, including a violin sonata, a *Romeo and Juliet* overture and an octet for piano, strings and wind, all written during 1873.) Certainly it coincided with an acceleration of change in his musical language. If the anguished tone of the String Quartet No. 5 in F minor, Op. 9 (B.37), written during September and early October 1873, reflects his disappointment at the shelving of his operatic hopes, it also demonstrates a new formal concentration. It is arguably the first work in which one can plainly recognise its composer's distinctive voice without undue benefit of hindsight, especially in the beautiful slow movement, which Dvořák subsequently arranged both for violin and piano and for violin and orchestra under the title

Romance (B.38 & 39). The third movement is a troubled waltz, over which the spirit of Schubert seems distantly to preside; and as in the last movement of the previous year's Piano Quintet, Czech elements come nearest the surface in the quartet's fiery finale. Two months later Dvořák laid down his pen on another string quartet, No. 6 in A minor, Op. 12 (B.40). This was originally conceived as a single-movement work with five distinct sections, but it is indicative of the changing direction of his musical thought that Dvořák reworked it into a more classically conventional four-movement form, evicting in the process a restlessly chromatic *Andante appassionato* in F major (B.40a). These creative struggles seem to have left him unsatisfied, and the A minor quartet remained unfinished (Jarmil Burghauser's reconstruction was published in 1979); but nowhere is it clearer than in this pair of chamber works from the closing months of 1873 that Dvořák's long musical apprenticeship was finally coming to an end.

The central work of this transitional year is Dvořák's Symphony No. 3 in E flat major, Op. 10 (B.34), which was completed shortly before he began work on the two quartets. Nearly eight years had elapsed since his Second Symphony, and again the advance is striking. The influence of Wagner is still evident in all three movements (it is Dvořák's only three-movement symphony), but the confidence exuded from the very first bars is now bolstered by the intense compositional experience of the intervening years. The symphony is not without flaws: the central section of the funereal slow movement sounds trite against the music around it, and the finale carries too little emotional weight for the rest of the work. But the audience who attended its premiere under Smetana at a Philharmonic concert on 29 March the following year could have been left in little doubt that the composer of the *Hymnus* was no one-hit wonder.

1873 marked a turning point in Dvořák's private life too. We do not know when he began an affair with Anna Čermáková, the now nineteen-year-old younger sister of his first love Josefina, but by the time rehearsals of *King and Charcoal Burner* ground to a halt she was already two months pregnant. The couple married on 17 November and moved in with Anna's parents. (The date seems to have been something of a Dvořák family tradition: his own parents had married on 17 November, and his daughter Otilie would marry the composer Josef Suk on her parents' twenty-fifth wedding anniversary.) Shotgun wedding or no, the marriage seems to have been a genuinely fulfilling one, and it provided the thirty-two-year-old composer with a stable home life for the first time since he had left the family hearth at Nelahozeves twenty years earlier. The appearance in print the same month of his first published work, a song called *The Lark* ('Skřivánek') (B.30/3), no doubt made an acceptable wedding present.

Dvořák's professional prospects may have been immeasurably brighter as a result of the events of 1873, but he was still living from hand to mouth. Teaching was now his main source of income, some of it coming from the well-to-do Prague merchant Jan Neff, who took the composer on as piano tutor to his young family at the beginning of the year; Dvořák seems also to have given lessons at a private music school. In February 1874 he took up his first regular job as organist since leaving the Organ School, at the church of St Adalbert (Svaty Vojtěch) in Prague; it was a post he held for the next three years, but the salary was less than half what he had received as principal viola in the Provisional Theatre orchestra. Somehow or other, though, the newlyweds managed to scrape together enough funds to set up house on their own. Shortly after the birth on 4 April 1874 of their first child, a boy they named Otakar, they moved into a rented flat

Bedřich Smetana in later life

at Na rybníčku (Teichgasse) in the New Town area of the city. And it was here, with the baby crying in the next room, that Dvořák knuckled down to the serious business of rewriting *King and Charcoal Burner*.

By now relations with Smetana, strained by his rejection of the first version of the opera, were clearly improving. Two months after giving the premiere of Dvořák's Third Symphony in March, Smetana also conducted the first performance of the scherzo from Dvořák's recently completed Symphony No. 4 in D minor, Op. 13 (B.41). Not performed in its entirety until 1892, by which time Dvořák had written his great Seventh Symphony in the same key, the Fourth is another transitional work. Perhaps strangely, given that Dvořák was finally pulling free of Wagner's gravitational field, the theme of the slow movement (Dvořák's first in variation form) is so Wagnerian as to seem permanently on the edge of breaking out into *Tannhäuser*. The scherzo, by contrast, is unreservedly Slavonic (and maddeningly catchy – one can see why Smetana thought it would go down well): marked *Allegro feroce*, its ferocity is that of a rather jaunty band of brigands. As so often in Dvořák's works of this period, the finale, here relentlessly over-exploiting a single rhythmic cell, is markedly the weakest movement.

In August Dvořák finished his rewriting of *King and Charcoal Burner* and resubmitted it to the management of the Provisional Theatre. It was accepted, and this time rehearsals went smoothly. On 24 November 1874 he finally had the satisfaction of seeing on stage a work that had gone through perhaps the most bizarre gestation of any opera in history. Certainly no one except the musicians who had worked on both versions could have guessed that this Weberesque 'number opera' had started life as a quasi-Wagnerian music drama. The first performance was conducted by Adolf Čech, Dvořák's old desk partner from St Cecilia Society days; Smetana had been forced to resign his conductorship of the Provisional Theatre in September when he was struck by sudden deafness, a symptom of the syphilis from which he would die a decade later. The premiere was a great success, but the opera failed to pull in the crowds thereafter and was taken off after three more performances. Dvořák always kept a soft spot for this first fruit of his operatic ambitions, and even its 1874 incarnation was to prove provisional: he reworked the score yet again for revivals in the 1880s.

The most significant event of 1874 for Dvořák's future career, however, was the application he made in July for a grant from the Austrian Ministry of Education. The Austrian State Stipendium was an annual award for indigent young artists of talent and always generated a bulging postbag for the jury, which included the Director of the Vienna Court Opera Johann Herbeck and the hugely influential Czech-born critic Eduard Hanslick. At thirty-three, Dvořák was stretching the definition of 'young', but he sent off to the Prague town clerk for a certificate confirming that:

Antonín Dvořák, teacher of music, born in 1841, married and father of one unprovided child, has no property, and that, except for a salary of 126 gulden which he receives as organist of the church of St. Adalbert and 60 gulden which he earns monthly by the private teaching of music, he has no other source of income.

This he duly despatched to Vienna with fifteen of his recent works, including symphonies (presumably Nos 3 and 4), overtures and the *Songs from the Dvůr Králové* [Queen's Court] *Manuscript* ('Pisně z Rukopisu Královédvorského') (B.30) – settings from the mysterious 'medieval' manuscript 'discovered' in the early nineteenth century and now regarded as an Ossian-style hoax. Among the manuscript's texts was 'The Lark', which had formed the material for Dvořák's first published song. Whatever the precise contents of the portfolio, the judges declared themselves impressed both with his 'undoubted talent' (however 'formless and unbridled' they found it in the symphonies and overtures) and with the fact that his choral and orchestral works had been performed at big public concerts in Prague. Early the following year he learnt that he had been awarded a grant of 400 gulden 'to ease his straitened circumstances and free him from anxiety in his creative work'– a windfall equivalent, if the town clerk's figures are to be believed, to more than twice his annual earnings. It was the first of five financial awards Dvořák would receive from the same source. It was also, just as importantly, his introduction to a group of powerful opinion-formers of the German-speaking musical world – including, from 1875, a new jury member who would be Dvořák's most distinguished advocate of all, Johannes Brahms.

While waiting for the result of the judges' deliberations, Dvořák composed in quick succession an orchestral Rhapsody in A minor, Op. 14 (B.44), which he later retitled *Symphonic Poem* ('Symfonická báseň'), and the String Quartet No. 7 in A minor, Op. 16 (B.45). The rhapsody was conceived as the first of a set of Slavonic rhapsodies – in the event it would be four years before Dvořák wrote any others – and is an early indicator of the national influences that would soon make themselves strongly felt in his music. In the quartet, by contrast, Dvořák was apparently trying to do *ab initio* what he had attempted from a different starting-point with his recently abandoned quartet in the same key: the work is one of his most conventionally Classical in form and, perhaps for this very reason, seems never quite to ignite. It was nonetheless the first of his chamber works to appear in print, the parts being published by the Prague publishing house of Emanuel Starý in 1875.

Encouraged by the acceptance of the second version of *King and Charcoal Burner*, Dvořák had also completed a one-act comic opera, *The Stubborn Lovers* ('Tvrdé palice'), Op. 17 (B.46), to a libretto written for him a few years earlier by yet another of Prague's literary lawyers, the young Josef Štolba. It tells the story of a country girl and boy, Lenka and Toník, whose parents, a widow and a widower respectively, want them to marry; but they will not admit their love for each other. They are tricked into revealing their true feelings by their benignly Mephistophelian godfather Řeřicha (a distant cousin of Mozart's Don Alfonso) when each is led to believe that their parent has designs on their beloved. Needless to say, all ends happily with Lenka and Toník falling into each other's arms. This neatly symmetrical tale inspired Dvořák to some of his sunniest music and the whole opera has an outdoor Bohemian charm; though it is not without moments of sudden emotional depth, such as Lenka's lovely aria 'Jak jest mi jen' ('What's wrong with me?') and Toník's almost Puccinian declaration of love in the climactic penultimate scene, 'V tobě já vidím blaho své' ('In you I see my happiness'). Its musical unity sounds perfectly natural, and there is scarcely a breath of Wagner. *The Stubborn Lovers* reached the stage only in 1881, and if its first-night audience did not leave the theatre whistling it, then the performance must have been even worse than the reviewers said.

Winning the stipendium seemed to open the floodgates for Dvořák, and 1875 saw an astonishing spate of creativity. When the news came through, he was working on his String Quintet in G major (B.49) (later misleadingly published as Op. 77), and the piece has an irresistible spring in its step: even the fire of the opening *Allegro con fuoco* sheds more light than heat. Recognisably Dvořákian throughout, with a hearty Czech scherzo and a finale in which Lenka and Toník seem not yet to have left the stage, this is the quintet through which part of the *Andante religioso* from the E minor String Quartet passed before ending up as a nocturne. It was begun for an Artistic Society chamber music competition and it duly won, though the prize money must by then have seemed small beer compared with the 400 gulden already in the composer's pocket.

Dvořák was now spending a lot of time with the Neff family, where he often played the piano while Jan Neff and his wife Maria sang. One such musical evening sowed the seeds of a work that would be instrumental in giving Dvořák his first access to an international audience. As Maria Neff remembered it:

We were specially fond of vocal duets which Dvořák obligingly accompanied. Only the limited choice annoyed us not a little. We got tired of the hackneyed repetition of Mendelssohn and other German composers. My husband, an ardent Moravian, once remarked to Dvořák in passing: 'Wouldn't it be possible to compose some duets from our own music, for instance from Moravian folksongs?' 'Why not?' – replied Dvořák. 'Look out for some nice texts and I shall do the rest.' ...Our governess borrowed Sušil's Collection [of Moravian national songs] and made her own selection of about fifteen songs. Dvořák promised to write a second part for them and a piano

accompaniment. In a few days, however, he announced that
he had changed his mind. 'I won't do that,' he said. 'If you like,
I'll write duets in my own way but I won't write a second part
for these things.'

Over the next couple of years Dvořák would write four sets
of *Moravian Duets* (B.50, 60, 62 and 69), several songs from
the second and third of which Neff arranged to have privately
published (as Op. 32) in 1876. Apparently without telling
Dvořák he also had some presentation copies bound, and sent
them to leading figures in Czech and German musical life,
including Hanslick and Brahms. Brahms had already made
a mental note of Dvořák's name when the latter put in his
second application for the Austrian State Stipendium in 1875,
and these duets made a deep impression on him, as the sequel
would show.

Compositions continued to pour from Dvořák's pen
during 1875. Shortly after writing the first set of *Moravian
Duets*, he finished the Piano Trio in B flat major, Op. 21
(B.51). The first of his four surviving piano trios, it is another
characteristic chamber work; spacious in conception, it has a
folksy swing to its opening *Allegro molto*, a limpidly unfolding
slow movement and a lively polka for a scherzo. There
followed hot on its heels the Serenade in E major for string
orchestra, Op. 22 (B.52), written in less than a fortnight in
May, and the Piano Quartet in D major, Op. 23 (B.53), begun
ten days later.

If the quartet is one of Dvořák's least revived pieces, the
serenade is one of his most enduringly popular. The earliest of
his compositions still to find a regular place in the concert hall
and recording studio, it is among the best-known works in the
Romantic canon and a staple of the string orchestra repertoire.
It has a directness and simplicity new to Dvořák's work. The

first of its five movements is a graceful *Moderato*, the second a lilting waltz whose sweeping trio melody provides the basis for the theme of the *Larghetto* fourth movement, a serenely contemplative *Nachtmusik*. Towards the end of the rollicking finale there is a marvellous interlude of peace as the work's opening theme returns.

CD 1 ②

The climax of Dvořák's creative activity in 1875 is the Symphony No. 5 in F major, Op. 76 (B.54), composed in just five weeks during June and July. The first great orchestral work of his maturity and the first of his symphonies still frequently programmed today, the Fifth marks a watershed in Dvořák's writing. The pastoral opening is one of the most magical of any symphony, while the perfectly paced slow movement, which is directly connected to the scherzo, has something of the character of a *dumka* (a type of Ukrainian lament, distinguished by alternating elegiac and lively sections, that Dvořák was to make peculiarly his own). The finale is Dvořák's most successful yet, a driven movement which begins not in the home key of F major but in a turbulent A minor, and ends with a glorious reminder of the opening theme of the whole symphony, now resplendent in the brass and conveying an exhilarating sense of homecoming. As the Dvořák scholar John Clapham has said, 'it is as if a new world is revealed in this symphony'. Throughout the work the richness of invention is matched by a mastery of form that points the way to the towering achievement of his last four symphonies.

Less than three weeks after finishing his symphony, Dvořák – never content for long without an opera in hand – began work on his most grandly conceived stage work to date. This was the five-act tragic opera *Vanda*, Op. 25 (B.55), the tale of a legendary Polish princess (cousin to the eponymous heroine of Smetana's *Libuše*) who throws herself into the Vistula in fulfilment of a religious vow when her country is saved from German invasion. Even by Dvořák's less than critical standards, the choice of a clunking libretto by Václav Beneš-Šumavský and František Zákrejs was a disaster. Composed between August and December 1875, the opera was a flop when it was mounted at the Provisional Theatre the following April, and after four performances it sank from sight almost as terminally as its unfortunate heroine. Dvořák's dramatic grip may be insecure across so broad a canvas, but *Vanda* nonetheless has its share of hidden treasures – the sublime quartet with chorus after the contest of the suitors in Act III, the heartfelt prayer of the High Priest and the people for victory in Act IV – and while its moment in the theatre may have passed, it remains among that virtual repertoire of operas whose most rewarding stage may after all be the recording studio.

While he was at work on *Vanda* Dvořák and his wife suffered the first of a sequence of tragedies that would strike at the heart of their family life during these years. Their second child, Josefa, was born on 19 September but died two days later. Even if the tone of his next two works, the Piano Trio in G minor and the String Quartet in E, are not, as commentators have tended to surmise, a reflection of Dvořák's state of mind in the aftermath of this loss, the fact that in the early months of 1876 he also sketched the *Stabat mater* – his first large-scale sacred work, and the classic Christian expression of a parent's grief at the death of a child – is surely suggestive of its impact. And it is unlikely to be a coincidence that Dvořák chose the same medium and key as Smetana had done some twenty years earlier when he dignified the death of his own daughter by producing a piano trio in G minor.

Whatever Dvořák's emotional condition in the autumn of 1875, the Piano Trio in G minor, Op. 26 (B.56) and the String Quartet No. 8 in E major, Op. 80 (B.57) breathe an unmistakable air of disquiet wholly at odds both with the tone of their immediate predecessors and with the upward trajectory of the composer's professional career at this time. The piano trio is an unsettling work, both for its intensity – the *Largo* slow movement is one of Dvořák's most affecting songs of yearning – and for the manner in which wraiths of the salon hover behind the music's prevailing desolation: the second subject of the first movement and the trio of the third, for example, seem to belong to a more polite world than the agitated material that frames them.

The String Quartet No. 8 in E major stands with the Fifth Symphony as a milestone in Dvořák's output: just as the Fifth is his first mature symphony, so this is his first fully mature quartet. The tone is inescapably elegiac: from the outset minor modes pervade the nominal E major. The slow movement belongs to the same emotional world as the *Largo* of the G minor Piano Trio; the wistfulness of the scherzo is only temporarily dispersed by the trio which, as in the G minor work, seems to belong to a more relaxed composition; and the finale, a more tightly constructed movement than the corresponding one in the piano trio, makes a worthy crown to the quartet as a whole. Both the trio and the quartet were composed in a white heat between 4 January and 4 February 1876, and the charming *Two Minuets* for piano, Op. 28 (B.58) written in their slipstream (and perhaps originally conceived as orchestral pieces) must have provided some much-needed light relief.

Several of Dvořák's remaining compositions in 1876 attest to his deepening interest in folk sources. The *Four Part-songs* ('Čtyři sbory') for mixed voices, Op. 29 (B.59), include a setting of two Moravian folk poems from František Sušil's enormously influential collection *Moravian National Songs* ('Moravské národní písně'), on which Dvořák had already drawn for his first *Moravian Duets* the previous year. This was also the source of the two sets of *Moravian Duets* he composed during 1876 (B.60 and 62), as well as the fourth set which he would write in 1877 (B.69). He quarried Moravian folk poetry again for two of the three *Choral Songs* ('Sborové písně') for male voices (B.66) from January 1877; the third song, Adolf Heyduk's 'The Fiddler' ('Já jsem huslař') provided the theme for one of Dvořák's greatest orchestral works, the *Symphonic Variations*, later the same year. His interest in folk poetry goes back at least as far as his *Four Songs on Serbian Folk Poems* ('Čtyři písně na slova srbské lidové poezie') (B.29) of 1872, but his increasing immersion in the folk literature and music of the Czech lands during the mid 1870s clearly marks a further step towards what is often referred to as his first Slavonic or national period.

One of the musical contacts to whom Procházka had opened the door for Dvořák was the Czech pianist Karel Slavkovský. A few years younger than the composer, Slavkovský was already a big name on the international circuit when Procházka had secured him to play in the premiere of the Piano Quintet, Op. 5 in 1872, and it seems to have been with a view to catching his imagination that in the summer of 1876 Dvořák composed his Piano Concerto in G minor, Op. 33 (B.63). If so, the speculation paid off: Slavkovský gave the first performance of the work, which was conducted by Adolf Čech, in Prague in March 1878. Whatever Slavkovský's view of it, however, few subsequent pianists have taken the concerto to their heart. Despite his training as a keyboard player, and later appearances at the piano to present his own chamber works, Dvořák seldom wrote as idiomatically for the piano as he did for strings. Several pianists have revised the piano part of the concerto, most notably Vilém Kurz of the Prague Conservatoire, in whose version it still tends to be

Dvořák, aged about thirty-six

played. Even so, the piece has never found a place in the front rank of Romantic piano concertos, partly perhaps because, despite having all the accoutrements of drama (especially in its outer movements) the work as a whole remains curiously lacking in dynamic tension.

There are indications that Dvořák himself was never happy with the concerto's piano part. However, he seemed reluctant to leave the keyboard after completing it and produced two other notable works for piano later the same year. The *Dumka* in D minor, Op. 35 (B.64) is significant as Dvořák's first use of a title to which his famous *Dumky* piano trio of 1891 would link his name in perpetuity, though in fact the piano piece is one of his less typical essays in the form. The final work of the year, the *Tema con variazioni* in A flat major, Op. 36 (B. 65) is a set of eight variations on a richly suggestive original theme and represents Dvořák's single most sustained contribution to the literature of the piano.

1877 dawned far brighter in the Dvořák household than had 1876. A new daughter, Růžena (Rose), had been born a few days after Dvořák completed the Piano Concerto, and his application for the Austrian State Stipendium had been successful for the third year running. This time the prize had gone up to 500 gulden (as befitting a portfolio that included the Fifth Symphony, the Piano Trio in G minor and the String Quartet in E major) and in February, three years to the day after he took it up, Dvořák resigned his post as organist at St Adalbert's. The same month, he started work on a new opera, *Šelma sedlák* (B.67).

Like *The Stubborn Lovers*, *Šelma sedlák* (usually translated as *The Cunning Peasant*) is a rambunctious slice of Bohemian rural life, but the libretto – by another of Dvořák's amateur playwrights, a rather messianic young medical student called Josef Otakar Veselý – has none of the tidiness of its predecessor.

The plot is a transparent conflation of *The Marriage of Figaro* and *The Bartered Bride* (from which two of the characters even take their names) and shows love triumphing over a superfluity of obstacles – the heroine, Bětuška, has no fewer than four suitors competing for her hand! Dvořák's music, however, has much of the same *plein air* sparkle as in *The Stubborn Lovers*, and if it cannot quite salvage the overpopulated plot, its unity papers over more of the cracks than Veselý had any right to expect. Dvořák is most beguilingly in his element in the opening scenes of Act II. It is a May evening, and in a local farmyard the village lads and lasses are making merry while the principals muse on their assorted hopes and plans in an extended sequence of choruses, dances and ensemble numbers which contain some of the opera's freshest as well as its most Slavonic music. As dusk falls, the young people carry the maypole back to the village inn, where they plan to continue their revelry until dawn – a scene surely drawn from Dvořák's Nelahozeves childhood. The strains of the polka fade into the distance and, in a finely graduated change of mood, Bětuška and her true love Jeník are left alone on stage in the failing light. Their tender love duet, and Bětuška's sudden unease when Jeník leaves her for the night, is one of few moments in the opera when the stock characters take on brief emotional life. *The Cunning Peasant* was a great success when it was premiered at the Provisional Theatre in January 1878. Four years later, in Dresden, it became Dvořák's first opera to be staged outside the Czech lands.

It was probably after finishing *The Cunning Peasant* that Dvořák treated himself to one of his rare vacations: a walking holiday with an intense young Moravian musician he had got to know in Prague. Leoš Janáček, then twenty-three years old, had graduated the previous year from the Prague Organ School, and was now eking out a living as teacher, conductor

*Leoš Janáček
in 1879*

and choirmaster back in Brno, where he had recently directed a performance of Dvořák's String Serenade. The two men struck up a friendship that would last for the rest of Dvořák's life. Janáček was a regular visitor to the Dvořáks' flat and an indefatigable champion of the older composer's music, with which his own output, for all its difference in musical language, reveals clear continuities. Since almost all the works for which Janáček is now celebrated were written after Dvořák's death, the influence is something of a one-way street, but there is no doubt that the friendship was one of deep mutual respect and shared aesthetic values. A flavour of that reciprocity is given by Janáček's often quoted tribute:

> *Do you know what it is like when someone takes the words out of your mouth as you are about to speak them? For me it was always that way in Dvořák's company. I can interchange his personality with his work: he also took his melodies from my heart. Nothing in the world can destroy such ties.*

After seeing Janáček, Dvořák visited another of his lifelong friends, Alois Göbl, whom he had met in his Provisional Theatre days but who had now given up a promising career as a singer in favour of teaching and administration on Prince Rohan's estate at Sychrov. He then returned to Prague, where, on 6 August, he began work on a new orchestral commission from Ludevít Procházka, the *Symphonic Variations*, Op. 78 (B.70). Exactly a week later his daughter Růžena, still less than a year old, was playing unsupervised in their flat when she drank a solution of phosphorus kept for making matches. She died soon afterwards. Less than four weeks later, the Dvořáks' only remaining child, three-year-old Otakar, died of smallpox. It was 8 September, Dvořák's thirty-sixth birthday.

It is impossible to reconstruct the emotions of parents who lost their children in an age of high and almost routine infant mortality. It is psychologically disorientating, for example, to reflect that the Dvořáks' fourth child was born nine months almost to the day after Otakar's death. A double blow in such circumstances was exceptional even by the standards of the time, however, and it must have strained the couple's resilience to the limit. Reserved to the point of taciturnity in personal matters, Dvořák left no verbal record of his feelings at this crisis. But for a composer used to working in the kitchen amid the racket of household life, and for whom his family was the emotional centre of existence, the silence of the suddenly childless Na rybníčku flat must have been hard to bear. Perhaps his and Anna's move to new accommodation at 10 Žitná (Korntorgasse) in November was partly intended as an escape from it. Significantly, it was also at this time that he returned to the sketches of his *Stabat mater*, written and set aside in the wake of his daughter Josefa's death two years earlier, and worked them up into full score.

Scored for choir, four soloists and orchestra, the monumental *Stabat mater*, Op. 58 (B.71) is the first major sacred work of Czech music. One of the most frequently performed pieces during Dvořák's lifetime, it was especially popular in England, where it would play a significant part in his future career. The penultimate number in particular, the contralto solo 'Inflammatus et accensus', seemed to strike a chord with audiences and was often performed separately from the rest of the cantata, although its almost Baroque figurations make it in some respects one of the less characteristic inspirations of Dvořák's maturity. Indeed, for all its undoubted force, the whole cantata is conspicuously free of the Slavonic tendencies surfacing in so much of his work during this period.

In its movement from the minor-key austerity of the first four numbers to the increasingly affirmative use of major keys in the last six, the music of the *Stabat mater* follows the movement of Jacopone da Todi's medieval poem from anguish and grief to the hope of redemption through suffering. No doubt it also reflects the course of the composer's own mourning. There is less evidence of grief, however, in the astonishing succession of compositions Dvořák produced during the months after the children's deaths than in the fact that writing them could hardly have allowed him an unoccupied moment. Between September and the end of the year, in addition to completing the *Stabat mater* and the *Symphonic Variations*, he turned once again to Czech and Moravian folklore for the *Bouquet of Czech Folksongs* ('Kytice z českých národních písní') for male voice choir, Op. 41 (B.72), produced a very un-Gaelic set of Scottish dances for piano (B.74; also confusingly designated Op. 41), and, in just eleven days in December, composed the String Quartet No. 9 in D minor, Op. 34 (B.75). Even leaving aside the fact that the cantata, the variations and the quartet are three of Dvořák's finest achievements, the sheer variety of this music would be remarkable at any time. In the wake of personal tragedy it represents an object-lesson in the independence of art and circumstance.

Whatever spiritual solace Dvořák derived from the musical expression of his faith in the *Stabat mater*, even while he was putting the finishing touches to the score a more worldly consolation was waiting in the wings. As in each of the previous three years, he had applied in 1877 for the Austrian State Stipendium. At the beginning of December a letter arrived from the spokesman of the judges, Eduard Hanslick. The news it contained was to signal a breakthrough in Dvořák's professional fortunes and to set him, a composer still barely known outside his homeland, on the high road to international acclaim.

Chapter 4

Nationalist and Internationalist (1877–1883)

The sympathy of an artist as important and famous as Brahms may be not only pleasant but also useful to you, and I think you should write to him... and perhaps send him some of your music.

Nationalist and Internationalist (1877–1883)

Hanslick's letter, dated 30 November 1877, informed Dvořák that he had once more been awarded the Austrian state prize, now fixed at 600 gulden. The stipend was starting to look like an annual paycheque, but if Dvořák was in any danger of becoming blasé about it the rest of the letter was calculated to set his adrenalin flowing again. Hanslick wrote that Brahms (who had sat on the panel of judges since 1875)

takes a great interest in your fine talent and likes especially your Czech vocal duets [Moravian Duets], *of which I too am exceptionally fond. The sympathy of an artist as important and famous as Brahms may be not only pleasant but also useful to you, and I think you should write to him... and perhaps send him some of your music. He has kept the vocal duets from your application materials in order to show them to his publisher and to recommend you to him. If you could procure a German translation, he would certainly arrange for their publication immediately. Perhaps send him a copy, and something from your manuscripts in addition – after all, it would be desirable for your things to become known beyond your rather narrow Czech fatherland, which in any case does nothing for you.*

Dvořák may have bristled at the slur on his country in the final sentence, but he was quick to act on Hanslick's advice. On 3 December he wrote to Brahms in Vienna.

Brahms could have been left in no doubt about Dvořák's gratitude for his offer of help: the tone of the letter is deferential to the point of obsequiousness. One typical sentence reads:

In that I implore Your Nobleness once more for your highly prized favour, to preserve the same for me also in future I ask at the same time for the gracious permission to be allowed to submit to you several of my chamber and instrumental compositions for your kind inspection.

Unlikely as it seems, this exercise in servility would mark the beginning of an enduring friendship, and one that was crucial to the spread of Dvořák's reputation throughout Europe and beyond.

On the face of it the differences between the two men outweighed their similarities. Brahms had yet to become the bearded patriarchal figure of popular image, but he was eight years older than Dvořák and already internationally established. He was German, a townsman, Protestant by background and freethinking by nature, a confirmed bachelor. Dvořák by contrast was proudly Czech, a countryman to his bones, a devout and apparently unquestioning Catholic, and a devoted family man. However, both were also outsiders, temperamentally reserved and unflamboyant. They both venerated the great masters of Viennese Classicism, and their musical training owed as much to the café or dance hall as it did to the academy. Over the years, their mentor–protégé relationship became a friendship of equals, based on genuine mutual esteem and uncompetitive support. Brahms's generosity to his younger colleague is particularly striking.

Johannes Brahms in 1876

He put his advice and his contacts freely at Dvořák's disposal, went out of his way to promote Dvořák's music in the German-speaking world, and even read his publishers' proofs for him when Dvořák was in the United States. He repeatedly tried, without success, to persuade Dvořák to move to Vienna in order to enhance his career prospects, on one occasion offering to pay his relocation and living expenses out of his own pocket. The two men met whenever they could, which was not often, and they seem to have relished each other's company. Above all, they held each other's music in the greatest respect. Brahms particularly admired his friend's fertility, once remarking: 'I should be glad if something occurred to me as a main idea that occurs to Dvořák only by the way'. When Brahms died in 1897 there were more scores by Dvořák in his library than by any other contemporary.

In the final months of 1877 all this lay in the future. But the single most important contribution Brahms made to Dvořák's life was arguably his first. As soon as he received Dvořák's letter he wrote to his own publisher, Fritz Simrock in Berlin, strongly recommending both the *Moravian Duets* and their composer:

> *Dvořák has written everything possible. Operas (Czech), symphonies, quartets, piano pieces. In any case he is a very talented man. And poor, besides! And I ask you to take that into consideration! The value of the duets will be obvious to you, and they might become a 'good commodity'.*

He furnished Simrock with Dvořák's address and at the same time wrote a typically no-nonsense letter to Dvořák himself, asking him to send the duets to Simrock and urging him to get them translated into German.

Dvořák clearly saw all this as the opportunity of a lifetime, and he did not let the grass grow under his feet. Within a fortnight he had despatched a German translation by Smetana's friend Josef Srb-Debrnov, and shortly afterwards set off on spec for Vienna to introduce himself to Brahms in person. The German master was away on a concert tour – how much fruitless travelling preceded the invention of the telephone! – but Dvořák called on Hanslick, who suggested he leave a portfolio of his compositions with Brahms's housekeeper instead. On his return to Prague, Dvořák followed up his abortive visit with a letter asking leave to dedicate to Brahms one of the works he had left at his house, the String Quartet in D minor. Events were starting to move with dizzying speed. Simrock had already agreed to publish the *Moravian Duets*, and by the time Brahms replied to Dvořák's letter the publisher had also commissioned the work that would transform Dvořák from a leading voice of Czech music into one of Europe's hottest musical properties: the *Slavonic Dances*.

Dvořák's relationship with Simrock, founded on Brahms's introduction and the runaway success of these dances, became an affectionate if not always wholly trusting one. Over the years, however, it would bring its share of frustrations for both parties. Simrock had a keen eye for the market, and as time went on his commercial requirements diverged ever more awkwardly from Dvořák's creative ambitions: 'light music' such as the *Slavonic Dances* was where the money was, not in string quartets or symphonies, and Simrock was unwilling to tamper with a successful formula. He was also as stubbornly German in his outlook as Dvořák was Czech in his. Such tensions not only led to periods of *froideur* between the two men, especially in the early 1890s, they also contributed to the chronological tangle which is the opus numbering of Dvořák's works: Simrock sought to pass off old works as new ones by giving them high numbers, while Dvořák tried to evade the contractual obligation to offer all his new works to Simrock by giving them low numbers and passing them off as old ones. For all its periodic difficulties, however, the relationship between composer and publisher remained a cornerstone of Dvořák's professional life right up to Simrock's death in 1901.

While Dvořák was avidly responding to these first overtures from Europe's wider musical community, his music was being heard ever more frequently at home. The *Symphonic Variations*, Op. 78 (B.70) had already been performed in Prague at the beginning of December 1877. A towering intellectual achievement, the succession of twenty-seven variations and finale pass like a review of the full panoply of Dvořák's talents. At the same time the music is never less than accessible, even its strictest procedures bearing the imprint of the composer's common touch. The finale, for example – a scurrying fugue – manages with perfect naturalness the unlikely transition from rigorous counterpoint to witty polka, and the work concludes with a resonant coda in which the future world of Bohuslav Martinů seems suddenly and unexpectedly close. The tonal and phrasal ambiguity of the theme, which is derived from the song 'The Fiddler' (one of the *Choral Songs* for male voices of January 1877), endows the unfolding variations with the multifaceted brilliance of a crystal held up to constantly shifting light.

As a showcase for Dvořák's extraordinary command of orchestral colour and mood the *Symphonic Variations* could hardly be bettered. It is all the more surprising, therefore, that after their first performance, in a little-noticed charity concert conducted by Procházka on Žofin Island, Dvořák seems to have consigned them to the shelf. Not until ten years later did he dust them off in response to a request for a new work for a concert in London. On first seeing the score, the conductor on that occasion, the redoubtable Hans Richter, wrote to the composer in frank bewilderment: 'It is a magnificent work! I am glad to be the first to perform it in London, but why have you kept it back so long? These Variations can take their place among the best of your compositions.' The audience clearly agreed. The work created a sensation: 'at the several hundred concerts which I have conducted during my life,' Richter reported to Dvořák afterwards, 'no *new work* has ever had such a success as yours.'

The early months of 1878 saw the successful premiere of *The Cunning Peasant* at the Provisional Theatre under the baton of Dvořák's old friend Adolf Čech, and the first performance of the Piano Concerto, with Slavkovský at the keyboard. Nor was there any slowing in the pace of Dvořák's creativity. In January he completed three part-songs for male choir entitled *From a Bouquet of Slavonic Folksongs* ('Z kytice národních písní slovanských'), Op. 43 (B.76), and less than two weeks later the Serenade in D minor, Op. 44 (B.77) for wind instruments, cello and double bass. Like its predecessor, the Serenade for strings, the wind serenade is a predominantly sunny work, a kind of Bohemian *concert champêtre*, its D minor a very different one from that of the String Quartet No. 9 or the later Seventh Symphony. It begins with a crisply ironic march, which, like the opening theme of the earlier serenade, returns as a familiar friend towards the end of the finale. An irresistible minuet follows, but the emotional centre of the serenade is the starlit *Andante con moto* with its shades of Mozart's similarly scored Serenade in B flat major (K.361), which Dvořák may have heard during his abortive visit to Vienna the previous month. In March he was nearing the end of his work on the first of a trilogy of *Slavonic Rhapsodies*, Op. 45 (B.86), when, with that serendipitous timing of which publishing successes are made, Simrock approached him with the commission for the *Slavonic Dances*.

A few days later, shortly after starting work on the dances, Dvořák received a reply from Brahms accepting the dedication of the String Quartet No. 9 in D minor. The older composer's letter is a characteristic mixture of gratitude and forthrightness:

> *...I shall merely say that to occupy myself with your things gives me the greatest pleasure, and that I should give a good deal to discuss individual points personally with you. You write rather hurriedly. When you are adding the numerous missing sharps, flats and naturals, then it would be advisable to look a little more closely at the notes themselves, and at the part writing, etc.*
>
> *Forgive me, but it is very desirable to point out such things. I consider myself honoured by the dedication of the quartet.*

It was a tone Dvořák knew how to appreciate, and he made several corrections and revisions to the score of the quartet. The resulting work, whose atmosphere of restless melancholy it is hard not to connect with the tragedies of the preceding summer, is among his finest essays in the form. The slow movement, in particular, is one of the most intensely felt in the quartet literature of the second half of the nineteenth century. Brahms wrote a subtly offhand letter to Simrock recommending the quartet, together with the String Quartet in E major from 1875:

> *I don't know what further risk you are wanting to take with this man. I have no idea about business matters or what interest there is for larger works. I do not care to make recommendations, because I have only my eyes and my ears*

and they are altogether my own. If you think of going on with
it at all, get him to send you his two string quartets, major and
minor, and have them played to you. The best that a musician
can have Dvořák has, and it is in these compositions.

But Dvořák was as yet an untested commercial proposition, and Simrock hung fire.

Things changed radically with the publication of the first set of *Slavonic Dances*, Op. 46. The eight dances were written for piano duet (B.78) from March to May, but Dvořák had already started orchestrating them before he finished the piano version, and three of them were given their first performance in orchestral guise at a concert in Prague conducted by Čech on 16 May. It was a review of the piano duet originals in a Berlin newspaper, however, which introduced the dances, and with them the name of Dvořák, to a wider European audience. Writing in the *Nazionalzeitung* in November, the influential music critic Louis Ehlert portrayed as a moment of revelation his discovery of this exciting new music: 'I was sitting one day in very bad humour buried in a heap of musical novelties... when suddenly two works, by a composer so far unknown to me, engrossed all my attention [the *Slavonic Dances* and the *Moravian Duets*]'. Ehlert briefly told his readers what little he had been able to discover of Dvořák's career to date. He then proceeded to describe the compositions in terms that must make this one of the single most transformative reviews in the history of music:

To put the matter shortly: Here at last is a hundred per
cent talent and, what is more, a completely natural talent.
I consider the Slavonic Dances *to be a work which will make*
its triumphant way through the world in the same way

as Brahms's Hungarian Dances*. There is no question here of some kind of imitation; his dances are not in the least Brahmsian. A heavenly naturalness flows through his music and that is why it is so popular. Not a trace of artificiality or constraint... Here we are confronted with perfected works of art and not perhaps with some pastiche stuck together from scraps of national melody... Whoever finds a jewel on the public highway is under obligation to report his find. I beg the reader to look upon these lines from that point of view.*

A few days later, in response to an appreciative letter from Dvořák, Ehlert was able to tell the composer that his review had 'produced a positive "run" on the music shops and, I can say without exaggeration, made you a name overnight'. Within months, the dances were being played in family drawing rooms throughout Europe and in public venues as far apart as Hamburg, Nice and London's Crystal Palace. By the end of 1879 they had even been performed in Boston, Massachusetts. At a stroke, the *Slavonic Dances* had done for Dvořák's international standing what the performance of the *Hymnus* had done for his reputation in Prague five years earlier. (It is worth noting, however, that they did little for his cash flow: Simrock had paid him nothing at all for the piano duet originals and only 300 marks for the orchestral versions. It was a red-letter day for Dvořák when the fee arrived – he took the envelope with him to show his friends at their local café – but it bears no relation to Simrock's turnover from the dances, which as Dvořák was quick to remind him in later years, proved to be a publishing goldmine.)

Much musicological ink has been spilt in tracing national models for the *Slavonic Dances*. Dvořák clearly drew on the dance forms he knew from his childhood – everyone agrees, for example, that the first and last dances are characterised by the exuberant swagger of the *furiant* – but he also cast his net more widely. The origins of some of the dances lie outside the Czech lands (as their generic title would suggest), and in others Dvořák combined features from different dance forms. He never dealt in direct quotation, any more than he was prepared simply to provide additional parts for existing songs in his *Moravian Duets* for the Neffs, but some of the dances do carry reminiscences of actual folk melodies. Ehlert was right, though, when he said in his review that the precise sources scarcely matter: what is extraordinary is the completely natural way in which Dvořák assimilates his originals to his own musical voice and the immediacy with which that voice speaks to the listener. The *Slavonic Dances* are occasional music of the highest and most engaging order, and the orchestral versions (B.83) have never lost their popularity. In one respect at least, Dvořák even came to regard them as something of a millstone round his neck: Simrock – his commercial judgement now vindicated in spades – spent the next eight years trying to squeeze a second set out of him.

Quite apart from its effect on Dvořák's public profile, Brahms's patronage seems also to have acted as a creative spur, each work seeding ideas for the next in rapid succession. Before he had even finished the *Slavonic Dances* he dashed off a wonderfully spontaneous set of five *Bagatelles* ('Maličkosti'), Op. 47 (B.79), for the unlikely combination of two violins, cello and harmonium. These happened to be the family resources available to the work's dedicatee, Josef Srb-Debrnov, at whose flat Dvořák often played the viola at quartet evenings (including one later in the year at which Smetana's First String Quartet 'From My Life' was first performed). The *Bagatelles* are a delightful thank-you letter to Srb-Debrnov for translating the *Moravian Duets* at such short notice a few months earlier.

A fortnight after finishing the *Bagatelles* Dvořák also completed the String Sextet in A major, Op. 48 (B.80). Like the *Bagatelles*, the sextet is recognisably the work of a composer immersed in Slavonic folk music. In the first movement the Schubert of the C major String Quintet (D.956) may seem to stand at his elbow, but its inflections are unmistakably those of Dvořák's homeland. After a bittersweet polka-cum-*dumka* movement, comes an energetic scherzo which (to the raised eyebrows of later musicologists) Dvořák designated a *furiant*. These two movements are among the most full-bloodedly Slavonic in all his chamber music; the trio of the latter even refers to the first of the *Slavonic Dances*. The finale is a set of five variations and *stretta* on an original theme. The critic Alec Robertson aptly described the sextet as having 'the effect of a brightly coloured travel poster' for the Czech lands. It certainly travelled, being the first of Dvořák's chamber works to be heard outside his own country – in Berlin one memorable evening the following summer at the home of the world-famous violinist Joseph Joachim. The sextet was a particular favourite of Brahms, who described it as 'endlessly beautiful'.

By the end of 1878 Dvořák had added two more *Slavonic Rhapsodies* to the one he had been working on when Simrock's commission for the *Slavonic Dances* arrived, rounding off a project heralded by the orchestral *Rhapsody* of 1874. Simrock snapped these up too, and though they never quite matched the popularity of the *Slavonic Dances*, they were soon being heard in an impressive sweep of concert halls from Dresden to Cincinnati. Dvořák himself conducted the premiere of the first two *Slavonic Rhapsodies* on Žofín Island on 17 November 1878 at a concert that was significant both for marking his fifth wedding anniversary and for being the first ever devoted entirely to his own music. It was the third rhapsody, though, with its echoes of 'Vyšehrad' from Smetana's *Má vlast*, that had the warmest reception during Dvořák's lifetime and has tended to be the one most often heard since. In addition to the *Slavonic Rhapsodies*, he also turned out a number of smaller works during the course of 1878: the virtuosic but rather empty *Capriccio* for violin and piano (B.81); a hymn for voice and organ, *Hymnus ad laudes in festo Sanctae Trinitatis* (B.82); *Three Modern Greek Songs* ('Tři novořecké básně') for voice and piano, Op. 50 (B.84); and two piano *Furiants*, Op. 42 (B.85), chips from the workbench on which the *Slavonic Dances* were fashioned.

Two events in Dvořák's private life during 1878 crowned what had been by any standards a momentous year. In June Anna gave birth to a daughter, Otilie, bringing the sounds of childhood back to their flat. (Otilie would unite two of the greatest names in Czech music by marrying the composer Josef Suk, whose grandson – also Josef Suk – was among the most celebrated violinists of the second half of the twentieth century.) Then in December Dvořák finally met the man who more than any other had made possible the transformation of the preceding twelve months, Johannes Brahms. It was perhaps to displace nervousness at the prospect of this first encounter with the German master that on the train to Vienna Dvořák kept himself busy by writing five choruses for male choir based on translations of Lithuanian song texts (B.87). If so, he need not have worried. According to the Prague music journal *Dalibor*, Brahms greeted him with open arms.

Over the months that followed, Dvořák found himself in ever greater demand as his star rose at home and abroad. Shortly after the first all-Dvořák concert in November 1878 he was made an honorary member of the prestigious Prague Hlalol (the choral society which had first performed his *Hymnus*, Op. 30), a harbinger of many honours to come, including soon afterwards the Chairmanship of the Music Section of the Artistic Society. Private individuals and public bodies approached him with commissions, including one for a new string quartet from Jean Becker, the leader of the well-known Florentine Quartet, and another for a setting of Psalm 149 from the Prague Hlalol itself. Publishers beat a path to his door, providing an instant outlet for old and new works alike. But it may not have been until the summer of 1879 that Dvořák realised the true extent of his fame outside the Czech lands. It was on 29 July that he visited Berlin and attended a musical evening at the apartment of Joseph Joachim, one of several distinguished figures on the European musical stage whose friendship he owed to Brahms. There his String Sextet and the work commissioned by Becker, the String Quartet No. 10 in E flat major, Op. 51 (B.92), were privately performed for the first time, and Dvořák, as he reported rather bemusedly to his friend Alois Göbl, 'spent among the foremost artists so many happy and agreeable moments that the memory of them will remain with me for the rest of my life'. To be the centre of attention for such internationally renowned musicians as Joachim could have left him in no doubt that the extraordinary reception of his *Slavonic Dances* had lifted him into a different public league.

Perhaps because this celebrity came fairly late to him, Dvořák always remained eminently level-headed about it. As Hanslick observed, he was 'as modest as he is talented'. There was never any question of resting on his laurels. In fact, to judge by his workload, there can have been little question of resting at all. In the early months of 1879 the writing of the String Quartet in E flat had been interrupted by a string of other compositions: a *Festival March* ('Slavnostní pochod') of rather hollow pomp and circumstance to mark the silver wedding of Emperor Franz Josef and Elizabeth of Austria

(Op. 53, B.88); two versions of a bracingly muscular *Mazurek* for violin and piano and violin and orchestra, Op. 49 (B.89 & 90); and for the Prague Hlalol, the Psalm 149 setting for male voices and orchestra (B.91), which was later revised for mixed voices and orchestra (B.154). There were also visits by Brahms and Simrock to accommodate, not to mention the premiere of the Fifth Symphony to attend – his first opportunity to hear a work he had composed almost four years earlier.

Except for the delay in completion, which meant that it missed his forthcoming Swiss tour, the String Quartet No. 10 in E flat amply satisfied Becker's desire for a 'Slavonic' work for his Florentine Quartet. It also confirmed, for all those now watching with close interest the products of Dvořák's pen, the promise of his String Quartet in D minor, and it remains among the most frequently performed of his quartets today. The first movement has an unforgettable breadth of perspective, a prospect, as it were, of Vienna from the woods and fields of Bohemia. Slavonic elements, the exoticism of which so appealed to new European audiences, make their most wholehearted appearance in the second movement, a *dumka* alternately languid and light-footed. They also occur in the finale, the main theme of which has some of the characteristics of a Czech 'leaping dance' or *skočná*. Nevertheless, these Slavonic features are fully integrated into a classicism with firm roots in the music of Mozart, Beethoven and Schubert.

Dvořák continued to mine the Slavonic seam with his *Czech Suite* ('Česká suita'), Op. 39 (B.93), probably written immediately after Becker's quartet. It is effectively the third panel in a triptych of serenades, of which the others are the String Serenade and the Wind Serenade. Scored for full orchestra, its five movements seem to look out on a less carefree Bohemia than that of the earlier works. The opening

'Praeludium' is a darkly mysterious pastorale over a drone bass, and there is a curious sense of oppression even in the more conventionally dance-like movements, the 'Polka' and the 'Sousedská (Minuetto)'. There was no long wait for first performances now, and the Suite was premiered by Čech in Prague on 16 May, 1879.

In the summer the Dvořáks stayed with Alois Göbl on Prince Rohan's estate in Sychrov. It may have been a holiday for one-year-old Otilie and her mother (who was now pregnant again), but even here Dvořák was as busy as ever. It was during this visit that he started drafting a work suggested to him by Simrock, the Violin Concerto in A minor, the completion of which, however, would prove an unusually long and layered process.

In the late autumn of 1879 Dvořák returned to the set of twelve piano miniatures, *Silhouettes*, Op. 8 (B.98), on which he had been working intermittently for the best part of a decade. In fact, their origins went back even further than that: these are the pieces that draw on his first two symphonies and the song cycle *Cypresses* – music of 1865, the year he fell in love with the woman who was now his sister-in-law, Josefina Čermáková. Was this just a reluctance to let good ideas go to waste, especially with publishers now hanging on his every note? Or did he feel the need, at a time of accelerating recognition, somehow to measure the distance he had travelled since his days as a struggling viola player? The genial, almost Straussian *Prague Waltzes* ('Pražské valčiky') for orchestra (B.99) and the Polonaise for orchestra in E flat major (B.100), written immediately after *Silhouettes*, are reminders of how well Dvořák could do 'light music' – despite his later dismissiveness towards the genre when dealing with Simrock. But they too seem touched with nostalgia for Komzák's band and his dance-hall days.

In October 1879, just as Dvořák was picking up the *Silhouettes* again, Brahms wrote to tell him that 'through rehearsals that have taken place you have won the sympathy of musicians here [in Vienna] to a quite extraordinary degree'. The following month Dvořák had a chance to experience that enthusiasm at first hand. On 16 November the Vienna Philharmonic Orchestra, under Hans Richter, gave the first ever performance of a Dvořák orchestral work in the Austrian capital. Two years younger than Dvořák, Richter was one of the most influential figures in the European musical world. A friend and supporter of Wagner, he had directed the first performance of the *Ring* cycle at Bayreuth three years earlier, and had just begun a series of annual concerts in London, which he would present until 1902. The work Richter selected to introduce Dvořák to the Viennese as an orchestral composer was the third *Slavonic Rhapsody*. Afterwards, Dvořák wrote what is by his phlegmatic lights a breathless account of the occasion to his friend Göbl:

I sat close to Brahms by the organ in the orchestra, and Richter drew me out. I had to appear. I must tell you that I immediately won the sympathy of the whole orchestra, and that out of all the new works they tried over, and Richter said there were sixty of them, they liked my Rhapsody *best of all. Richter embraced me on the spot, and told me he was glad to know me, and promised that the* Rhapsody *will be repeated at an extra concert in the Opera House.*

More lionising was to follow:

On the day after the concert Richter gave a banquet at his house, in my honour so to say, and invited all the Czech members of the orchestra. It was a splendid evening that I

shall not easily forget for the rest of my life. It was something
like the one in the summer at Joachim's.

There is some evidence, though, that the audience at the concert was not quite as ecstatic as the orchestra – a bellwether perhaps of the deteriorating relations between Vienna and Prague that would cloud reception of Dvořák's music in Austria during the next decade. There are two other pointers to the future in Dvořák's letter to Göbl. He writes that he has promised to send the Philharmonic a new symphony for their next season, an assurance that sowed the seeds of his Sixth Symphony. And a jaunty postscript records the interest of the Vienna Court Opera Director in Dvořák's opera *Vanda*: 'That would top everything if they were to perform my opera in Vienna! What?!' Nothing came of the idea, but it is a reminder that opera was seldom far from Dvořák's thoughts. It had been two-and-a-half years since *The Cunning Peasant*, during which time he had commissioned and toyed with a libretto on the Czech legend of Šárka. In the event he lost interest in the project – Janáček later co-opted the libretto for his own opera on the subject – but it would not be long before he turned to the stage again. The result would be one of the central works of his so-called Slavonic period, the historical opera *Dimitrij*.

Dvořák began work on his Sixth Symphony in the August after his momentous visit to Vienna. In the meantime he revised the work that he had started at Sychrov the previous summer, the Violin Concerto in A minor, Op. 53 (B.108). Dvořák had been discussing the concerto on and off with Joachim since their first meeting in Berlin, and in December 1879 the great virtuoso had gratefully accepted the dedication of the work. Once he had had a chance to look at it in more detail, though, he suggested numerous changes, which Dvořák implemented in the spring of 1880. In the process he made a thoroughgoing revision of the original score, as he outlined to Simrock in a letter that has about it something of the schoolboy reporting to the headmaster's study:

According to Mr Joachim's wish, I worked most carefully over the whole concerto, without missing a single bar. He will certainly be pleased by that. I put the greatest effort into it. The whole concerto has been transformed.

Nor was this the end of the matter. Joachim sat on the manuscript for an unconscionably long time before suggesting further changes, which Dvořák dutifully made. By the time the publishers weighed in with their own proposals – Simrock's right-hand man objected to the work's most

Fritz Simrock, Dvořák's principal publisher

innovative feature, the fact that the first movement is truncated and linked directly to the second – the composer had clearly had enough and dug in his heels. After all this toing and froing, Joachim never actually played the concerto: when the first performance finally took place, in October 1883, it was given by the elegant young Czech violinist František Ondříček, who several years earlier had played in the first performances of the String Quintet in G major (B.49) and the Piano Trio in B flat major (B.51). Unlike the Piano Concerto, and partly no doubt because of Joachim's advice, the

Violin Concerto has never attracted the remedial attentions of later soloists. Like the earlier work, however, it has never quite made it to the top table of nineteenth-century concertos for its instrument, despite its many beauties, which include in the slow movement some hauntingly limpid dialogues between solo violin and woodwind. The finale, a joyfully headlong sonata rondo, is the most conspicuously Slavonic of the three movements.

By contrast, there has never been any doubt about the centrality to the nineteenth-century symphonic repertoire of Dvořák's Symphony No. 6 in D major, Op. 60 (B.112). It had been five years since the Fifth Symphony signalled Dvořák's full maturity as a composer, and the new symphony is the first of his four undisputed masterpieces in the form. The Sixth has often been compared with Brahms's Second Symphony of 1877, which is in the same key, but it is rather Beethoven's spirit which most informs the work, especially in the first movement and the rapt *Adagio* – surely a conscious homage to the slow movement of Beethoven's 'Choral' Symphony. Whatever his influences, however, Dvořák is entirely himself throughout, and the scherzo that follows – a whirling *furiant* in which village square and concert hall converge without the slightest sense of incongruity – is one of his most characteristic inventions. The whole symphony is the work of an artist at the height of his powers, and Richter was so delighted when Dvořák played it through for him on the piano in November that he embraced the composer after every movement. In the event, however, it was not Richter in Vienna but Čech in Prague who gave the first performance, on 25 March 1881. The scheduled (and rescheduled) Vienna premiere fell foul of the city's cultural chauvinism – two Czech works in two seasons proved one too many – and Richter, having failed to pilot the work he had commissioned through the shoals of

Austrian musical politics, had to be satisfied with the honour of the dedication instead. The symphony was Dvořák's first to be published, in 1882, and Simrock, who seldom let respect for chronology hinder his marketing, called it No. 1. (None of the first four symphonies appeared in print until after Dvořák's death, and the Fifth was published only after the Seventh, which Simrock therefore called No. 2, the Fifth becoming No. 3. These numerical convolutions have long since been straightforwardly resolved in favour of numbering by order of composition.)

Apart from the Violin Concerto and the Sixth Symphony, 1880 saw an amiable, if not always distinguished, profusion of smaller works, in most of which the keyboard plays a part. In January, the same month in which Anna gave birth to her second surviving child (also called Anna), Dvořák supplemented his five *Prague Waltzes* for orchestra with a charming set of eight *Waltzes* for piano (B.101); the first, with its halting main theme, and the fourth, a more spirited turn round the dance-floor, he also arranged for string quartet or string orchestra (B.105). Other works for piano followed during the course of the year: a set of four *Eclogues*, Op. 56 (B.103), the last of which prefigures by several years themes used in the first number of the second set of *Slavonic Dances*, Op. 72; a set of four *Album Leaves* ('Lístky do památníku') (B.109); six *Piano Pieces*, Op. 52 (B.110), the second a tolling Intermezzo whose sadness seems to break the bounds of the salon; and six *Mazurkas*, Op. 56 (B.111), the fifth of which is derived from the first of the *Eclogues*.

More substantial than the works for solo piano are the song cycle and the violin sonata Dvořák composed during the first quarter of 1880. The *Gypsy Melodies* ('Zigeunermelodien') for voice and piano, Op. 55 (B.104), seven settings of poems by Adolf Heyduk, make less play of gypsy colouring than might have been expected, but are among Dvořák's most successful vocal works. The fourth of the set, 'Songs my mother taught me' ('Als die alte Mutter'), has become probably his most famous song. Exceptionally for Dvořák, the poems are in German: the songs were written for a singer at the Vienna Court Opera, and Heyduk translated his Czech originals for the purpose. This, and the fact that Simrock published the *Moravian Duets* only in German translation, was the subject of some bitter comment in the Prague musical press, which even questioned whether Dvořák wanted 'to remain one of us'. No doubt such polemics increased Dvořák's determination not to let his Bohemian identity be eroded by his Teutonic connections: he persuaded Simrock to publish the songs in Czech the following year.

Fielding one of Simrock's regular requests for another set of *Slavonic Dances* in February 1880, Dvořák, fresh from a visit by Brahms and Joachim, wrote: 'I feel now the need to write something serious. A Trio or a Violin Sonata – that would be what I shall need to keep me in good humour.' The trio did not materialise until much later, but the Sonata for Violin and Piano in F major, Op. 57 (B.106) was written the following month. Joachim played it through with Dvořák in Berlin at the end of March and gave it his blessing, despite (or perhaps because of) the fact that, unusually, the Brahmsian accents of the first movement seem almost to submerge Dvořák's personal voice. Brahms must also have been much on Dvořák's mind towards the end of the year. At Simrock's request, he orchestrated five of Brahms's *Hungarian Dances* in the early days of November, before visiting the great man himself later in the month while in Vienna to deliver the Sixth Symphony to Richter. A couple of weeks later he rounded off 1880, as he had 1879, with another orchestral dance, the beer-slopping *Polka 'For*

Prague Students' ('Polka "Pražským akademikům"') (B.114).

This flurry of writing contributed handsomely to the Dvořák coffers. Simrock paid a total of 2,800 marks for the *Waltzes*, the *Gypsy Melodies* and the Violin Sonata – more than nine times what he had paid for the *Slavonic Dances* only two years earlier – and other publishers bought what Simrock left, Hofmeister of Leipzig and Bote und Bock of Berlin adding the *Piano Pieces* and the *Mazurkas* respectively to their growing catalogues of Dvořák keyboard music.

In May 1880 the Dvořáks were able to move from the back to the front of the building in Žitná where they had lived since 1877. The airier new apartment, on the second floor and facing the street, would remain their Prague home for the rest of the composer's life. Two months later Dvořák took his first holiday at Vysoká in southern Bohemia, which was to become his much-loved second home; the Vysoká estate belonged to his brother-in-law Count Kounic, who in 1877 had married Josefina Čermáková. Amid these broadening prospects, there was also a reminder of the more distant past. In September, while he was still at work on the Sixth Symphony, Dvořák visited Zlonice to take part in a charity concert to raise money for a memorial to his old teacher Antonín Liehmann, who had died the previous year at the age of seventy-one – a touching tribute to the man who had first set him on the path to musical success, and testimony to that loyalty to his own humble roots much noticed by Dvořák's contemporaries.

Just as the Violin Concerto and the Sixth Symphony relegated other work to the (profitable) sidelines in 1880, so for most of the next two years a single major composition, the historical grand opera *Dimitrij*, Op. 64 (B.127), absorbed almost all Dvořák's creative energies. For much of the twentieth century critics tended to regard Dvořák's commitment to opera as at best an unfortunate distraction from work more suitable to his talents, and at worst a kind of pathological compulsion. In reality it was a natural outgrowth of his desire to write music that both connected with popular taste and expressed what he saw as the national spirit of his people. As he told an interviewer in the last year of his life: 'I consider opera the most advantageous of genres for the nation... Large sections of society hear such music, and hear it very often.' For all its Ministry of Culture tone, there can be little doubt that this reflects Dvořák's attitude throughout his life.

Never were opera and the aspirations of the Czech people so closely identified as in 1881. It was in that year that the great National Theatre project, which had muddled along for nearly two decades in temporary accommodation at the Provisional Theatre, finally came of age. A permanent home, funded by public donations – 'a gift from the nation to itself', as the inscription over the proscenium movingly read – was now nearing completion on the Vltava Embankment, and its inauguration was scheduled for later in the year. In January 1881 Jan Nepomuk Maýr, who had returned to the conductorship of the Provisional Theatre after Smetana's forced retirement, showed Dvořák a libretto that was originally intended for his fellow Czech composer Karel Šebor. Not surprisingly, Dvořák's imagination was fired by its fiercely Slavic message.

Dimitrij – a treatment of the story of the false Demetrius, who claimed to be the son of Ivan the Terrible and succeeded Boris Godunov on the Russian throne – was indirectly based on a dramatic fragment by Schiller. It thus takes up the story where Mussorgsky left off at the end of *Boris Godunov*, an opera Dvořák would not have known. There was something else Dvořák did not know, as a diary entry from the twenty-eight-year-old librettist reveals:

[Maýr] *came with the news that Dvořák liked* [the libretto] *very much and had asked Maýr if he could speak with the gentleman librettist. Maýr, who had not at first divulged whom the libretto was by, replied that the librettist wore skirts...*

Marie Červinková-Riegrová was the daughter of František Ladislav Rieger, leader of the Old Czech party. It was not her gender, however, but her political connections that gave Dvořák pause for thought. In particular, Smetana was at daggers drawn with Rieger, and Dvořák hesitated before entering what, in the feverish atmosphere surrounding the inauguration of the National Theatre, threatened to be a minefield of domestic cultural politics. In the end, after taking advice, he decided to go ahead, and began discussions with Červinková-Riegrová. It was a sound decision. Červinková-Riegrová was no Da Ponte, but she was by far the most capable of all Dvořák's librettists, and *Dimitrij* was to prove his finest opera to date.

The composition of *Dimitrij* occupied Dvořák almost continuously from May 1881 to September 1882, nearly everything else he wrote at the time being fitted in around it. In March 1881, before he began work on the opera, he completed ten *Legends* ('Legendy') for piano duet, Op. 59 (B.117), orchestrating them at Simrock's request later in the year (B.122). Modelled to some extent on the *Slavonic Dances*, not least in being presented to the public in both duet and orchestral guise, the *Legends* are not, despite their title, programmatic pieces. Rather, they are a series of mood pictures, the more meditative of which can tend towards the amorphous, especially in their orchestral form which sometimes smudges the clarity of the original; against expectations, therefore, the piano duet versions can often seem the more colourful. Dedicated to Hanslick, the *Legends* have had their devotees, including Brahms, who envied their composer his 'fresh, cheerful and rich resourcefulness', but they failed to reproduce the success of the *Slavonic Dances*, in either the drawing room or the concert hall.

The most significant work of 1881, however, is the String Quartet No. 11 in C major, Op. 61 (B.121). Dvořák's last quartet before the famous (and very different) 'American' Quartet of 1893, it was commissioned by Joseph Hellmesberger, another of those musical luminaries whom Brahms had enthused about Dvořák's work. Leader of both the Vienna Court Opera and an eponymous quartet, Hellmesberger had given public performances of the String Sextet in Austria in the spring of 1881 and was keen to have a new quartet for his next season. Dvořák began writing in October, working on *Dimitrij* in the mornings and the quartet in the afternoons, but made a completely false start (the Quartet Movement in F major, B.120, is his abandoned opening movement). He began all over again, but had only written three movements when he read in the newspaper in November that on 15 December Hellmesberger would be holding a concert to perform the quartet – 'which still doesn't exist!' he wrote to Göbl, with a mixture of amusement and exasperation at having to redirect his resources from the opera score. The quartet shows no signs of haste, however. If anything, it feels a little too worked – as if, despite his Czech pride, Dvořák was uncomfortably conscious, even awed, at the prospect of writing a string quartet for Vienna, the spiritual home of the form. In later years, with the eccentricity that marked his teaching methods, Dvořák would adjure his students to kneel when listening to Beethoven, and there is something of the constraint of genuflection about this music too. While it may be the least characteristic of Dvořák's mature quartets, however, there is still no one else's work for which it could realistically be mistaken.

As it turned out, there was no need for him to have hurried: Hellmesberger's December concert was postponed when fire gutted Vienna's Ringtheater, and the quartet had to wait almost a year for its first performance. It was, strangely, a season of theatre fires. In August, just two months after its ceremonial inauguration with a performance of Smetana's long-withheld festival opera *Libuše*, the new National Theatre in Prague had also burned down. After so many deferred hopes, the catastrophe caused a sense of national bereavement, but it also lifted any remaining pressure Dvořák may have felt over meeting his original timetable of completing *Dimitrij* for the autumn season's opening. As a happy counterweight to his own part in the patriotic mourning, his daughter Magda was born five days after the fire.

At the turn of the year Dvořák wrote two sets of songs for voice and piano (B.123 & 124) – his first significant reworkings of the *Cypresses* cycle of 1865. He also composed an overture and incidental music to František Ferdinand Šamberk's play *Josef Kajetán Tyl*. Tyl, an early nineteenth-century Czech playwright, wrote the words of the song *Where is my homeland?* ('Kde domov můj?'), which in František Škroup's popular setting was adopted as the joint national anthem of Czechoslovakia in 1918 and the national anthem of the Czech Republic in 1993. Dvořák's overture, which makes great patriotic play of Škroup's tune, survived the demise of Šamberk's drama to become a concert piece under the title *My Home* ('Domov můj'), Op. 62 (B.125a). All this was a theatrical siding for Dvořák, however, and after writing (in just three days) settings for mixed voices of five Hálek poems (B.126) under the title *In Nature's Realm* ('V přirodě'; not to be confused with the 1891 concert overture of the same name), he was able to get back on track with the full score of *Dimitrij*. Free of further interruptions, he put the final touches to it on 23 September 1882; the first performance, conducted by his old flatmate Mořic Anger, took place just fifteen days later in the New Czech Theatre, a short walk from Dvořák's house in Žitná.

Červinková-Riegrová's libretto gave Dvořák ample scope to show his operatic wares in dramatic confrontations, great set-piece crowd scenes and moments of high pathos. But the music of *Dimitrij* is pervaded above all by an atmosphere of claustrophobia broodingly evocative of the cloak-and-dagger world of Russian court politics. A handful of leitmotifs bind the work together, the two most important being stated at the beginning of the overture: a dramatically ominous theme associated with Dimitrij himself, and an oddly desolate one associated with the pure-hearted Xenie, Boris Godunov's daughter, with whom Dimitrij falls in love. Psychological (if unhistorical) tension is provided by the fact that for most of the action Dimitrij genuinely believes himself to be the rightful heir to the throne. This adds immense force to the opera's most dramatic crisis: in the final scene Ivan's widow Marfa hesitates before the holy cross, undecided whether to swear that Dimitrij is her son, while he, having learnt the truth from Marina, his spurned Polish wife, urges Marfa not to perjure herself for him. Perhaps the most beautiful moment in the whole work, however, is Xenie's Act II lament at her father's tomb, 'Baťusko můj' ('Oh my father'), which becomes a duet with the hidden Dimitrij after Xenie hears an approaching party of Poles offstage. Xenie's lamentation motif recurs in Dimitrij's tormented love aria 'Viděl jsem ji' ('I have seen her'), which begins Act III. Omens and desolation open the fourth and final act of the opera too, in Xenie's soliloquy 'Mně zdálo se, ž smrt bledá' ('I dreamt that pale Death'), with its repeated 'Běda' ('Alas'). For all the rousing 'national' music given to the choirs representing the opposing Polish and Russian factions,

85

it is these moments of personal anguish that remain in the mind after the crowds have left the stage, and which give the opera its enduring power to move.

The eminent critic Kurt Honolka has memorably described *Dimitrij* as Dvořák's 'problem child'. The composer lavished great love on it, defending it angrily against criticism and longing to persuade the world at large to share his affection for it. He nonetheless repeatedly revised the score in response to his and others' perceptions of its shortcomings, creating in the process a textual morass which has itself inhibited revivals. *Dimitrij* was a triumph at its premiere and became a staple of the repertoire in the Czech lands, clocking up some fifty performances in the next decade; but Dvořák was deeply disappointed in his lifelong wish to see it adopted internationally. It was performed abroad only once during his lifetime, when the National Theatre company mounted it at the International Exhibition in Vienna in 1892, and not until the second half of the twentieth century was it staged again outside his homeland.

Dvořák's frustrations over *Dimitrij* were symptomatic of a deeper tension during this period between his ambitions as a national and an international composer. Relations between the Czech- and German-speaking peoples of the Habsburg Monarchy deteriorated sharply during the 1880s, at just the time when Dvořák was starting to be seriously courted by German musical organisations. The Director of the Vienna Court Opera, Franz Jauner, was making preparations to stage *The Cunning Peasant* and had bought the Viennese performing rights to *The Stubborn Lovers*, and, though neither work finally made it to the stage in the Austrian capital, *The Cunning Peasant* brought the house down in Dresden in 1882 at a performance attended by the Queen of Saxony. Jauner was also sounding out Dvořák about writing a German opera specifically for Vienna. Hanslick was exerting pressure in the same direction, writing to Dvořák in June 1882: 'After such great initial successes, your art requires a wider horizon, a German environment, a bigger, non-Czech public.' Meanwhile the Czechs were asserting their independence at home with greater determination than at any time since the cultural revival of the 1860s. On the one hand, an opera commission from the most prestigious company in Austria – with the certainty of performance in Vienna – would have set the seal on the reputation Dvořák had already acquired outside the Czech lands since the launch of the *Moravian Duets* and the *Slavonic Dances*. On the other hand, he saw opera precisely as the *vox populi* of an oppressed nation, and one with which he felt his solidarity now more keenly than ever. Already torn between the promise of Hanslick's 'wider horizon' and loyalty to his homeland at a time of nationalist ferment, he was further shaken by the death of his mother in Kladno on 15 December 1882.

It was against this troubled background that Dvořák created one of his greatest works, the Piano Trio No. 3 in F minor, Op. 65 (B.130). Composed between 1 February and 31 March 1883, the trio is unlike anything Dvořák had written before in its fusion of emotional intensity and rigorous formal control, and the surviving manuscripts show that it was the outcome of considerable trial. The first movement is built on an almost symphonic scale, and there is little relaxation of the emotional tension even in the ensuing scherzo, while the ternary slow movement has the purposeful stillness of profound meditation. The landscape of the finale abuts the passionate territory of the opening movement, but there is now the promise of dancing too, and the music's breakthrough into the major mode at the end rings with the conviction of a hard-won struggle. Looking ahead to the great Seventh

Symphony of 1885, the piano trio stands at the threshold of a new – and, in its musical language, more universal – phase of Dvořák's creative life.

Something of the tensions of this period also leaked into the tonally unsettled piano miniature he completed just before starting work on the piano trio: the *Impromptu* (B.129). Biographically conditioned readings aside, however, it would be hard to find more than a passing shadow in the work Dvořák composed immediately after the trio, the spirited *Scherzo capriccioso* for orchestra, Op. 66 (B.131). Such volatility of mood as it exhibits falls within the healthiest of ranges, touching exhilaration at one end and seldom plumbing depths darker than mischief at the other. Čech gave the *Scherzo capriccioso* its first public airing in Prague

The National Theatre, Prague

a fortnight after it was finished, and it soon became one of Dvořák's best-travelled concert pieces.

In the summer of 1883 the Director of the National Theatre, František Adolf Šubert, approached Dvořák to compose the music for a projected trilogy of plays about the Hussite wars. Not surprisingly, given his patriotic heart-searching at this time, the composer leapt at the opportunity, and by 9 September he had completed his *Hussite Overture* ('Husitská'), Op. 67 (B.132) – in the event the only part of Šubert's project to get off the starting block. The Bohemian religious reformer Jan Hus, who was burnt at the stake in 1415, was widely seen in the Czech lands as a champion of national rights against ecclesiastical and temporal oppression. His potency as a symbol of Slavonic pride was greater than ever in the nationalist 1880s, and Dvořák built his overture around two themes which formed a kind of musical bedrock for the Czech sense of identity: the Hussite chorale and battle-hymn 'Ye who are God's warriors' ('Ktož jsú boží bjovníce') – which Smetana had used so memorably in *Tábor* from *Má vlast* – and the early medieval Wenceslas chorale ('Svatý Václave'). The *Hussite Overture* is infused with all the drama and nobility of the historical events that underpin its nominal programme. Dvořák encountered some Catholic objection to his use of such quintessentially Protestant material, but for most Czechs the Hussite cause transcended religious divides as completely as the music transcended political ones. Hans von Bülow was a German champion of the work, and it was partly his tireless support that led Dvořák to dedicate his Fifth Symphony to him. It is interesting to note, though, that exceptionally among Dvořák's scores there is no 'Bohu díky' at the end of the autographs of the *Hussite Overture*, the *Scherzo capriccioso* or the F minor Piano Trio – a hint that the self-questioning of this period may have permeated the deepest levels of his inner life.

The composer's crisis of conscience remained unresolved when the rebuilt National Theatre opened in November 1883, an occasion marked by a national holiday and the first performance of the *Hussite Overture*. There was no gainsaying the overture's authentic patriotism, especially on an occasion so imbued with national spirit, but Dvořák had still not conclusively rejected the German road to glory represented by the advances of Jauner and Hanslick. It would be some years before he was able to negotiate to his own satisfaction a path between his responsibilities as a nationalist and his aspirations as an internationalist. But by the time the first-night audience heard his rousing tribute to the spirit of the Czech people a new horizon had already opened to him in an unexpected direction.

Dvořák's music had been played in England since at least as early as February 1879, when August Manns had presented three of the *Slavonic Dances* at the Crystal Palace. In March 1883, however, the organist, conductor and composer Joseph Barnby gave the first English performance of the *Stabat mater* at the Royal Albert Hall. England's long-cherished choral traditions made fertile territory for the cantata's foursquare spirituality, and critics and audience alike took the work to their hearts. It seems to have been Barnby's concert that prompted the Philharmonic Society of London to write to Dvořák. In August he received a letter from the society's secretary, Henry Hersee, informing him 'that at the last Meeting of the Directors of this Society, it was unanimously resolved that "Herr Dvořák be invited to produce an orchestral selection (Suite or Overture) during the Society's Seventy-second Season (1884)"' and that the concerts would take place from February to May. Hersee continued:

I shall therefore be glad to be favoured by you with an early reply stating whether you can accept this Invitation of the Directors and whether it would be agreeable to you to attend the Concert and conduct the performance of the work.

To such impeccably bureaucratic strains did the curtain rise on a new and decisive phase of Dvořák's professional life.

Chapter 5

The English Triumphs (1884–1891)

He had never been to sea before,
and had no more than a few words
of phrasebook English.

The English Triumphs (1884–1891)

Dvořák's visits to England were the most revelatory experience of his career. In all, he made eight trips between 1884 and 1891, and a ninth in 1896. In the process, he established a new and profoundly appreciative audience for his music and laid the foundations for his later groundbreaking adventure in the English-speaking world: his residency in America. The extraordinary enthusiasm with which he was greeted in England astonished and delighted him. It also gave him a new self-confidence, the effects of which can be seen in his dealings with Simrock and other professional contacts in the years that followed. Above all, England offered Dvořák a route to wider recognition that bypassed the thorny political path through German-speaking Europe.

Whether or not he saw things in that light at the time, he promptly accepted the Philharmonic Society's invitation and made arrangements to travel to London in March 1884. Within months, he acquired a second string to his English bow when he was approached by the publishing house Novello, Ewer and Co., who had heard of his plans. Alfred Littleton, the son of Novello's owner Henry Littleton, wrote to ask if Dvořák could also conduct the *Stabat mater* during his forthcoming visit and whether he might be interested in writing a choral work for an unspecified festival the following year. After clearing matters with the Philharmonic Society,

Dvořák accepted Littleton's invitations too and sold Novello the world rights to the work for a mouthwatering 5,000 marks. (For comparison, Simrock had paid 2,000 marks for the Sixth Symphony; London was proving profitable before Dvořák had even left home.)

To the British press Dvořák would soon be 'the Bohemian Brahms'. In the meantime, while finalising his arrangements for England, Dvořák was seeing more than usual of the German original. In October he visited Vienna, and spent the middle and end of every day with Brahms, writing to Simrock in uncharacteristically rapturous terms of his devotion to the older composer. Brahms had just finished his Third Symphony and played him the first and last movements, which Dvořák (whose critical vocabulary tended to the abstract) described as 'pure love'. He was back in the Austrian capital in December for the premiere of the symphony, which shared a programme with his own Violin Concerto, here receiving its first Viennese performance at the experienced hands of Ondříček. In January 1884 he met Brahms again in Berlin, where the latter was conducting a performance of the symphony himself.

Earlier in the month Dvořák had dealt with the last commission on his desk before his departure for England. Ever looking to repeat the success of the *Slavonic Dances*, Simrock had asked him for another set of piano duets. *From the Bohemian Forest* ('Ze Šumavy'), Op. 68 (B.133) is the sort of music Dvořák could turn out with his eyes closed, but inspiration failed him when it came to titles for the six individual items. Complaining that Schumann had taken all the best ones, he appealed for help to Marie Červinková-Riegrová, his *Dimitrij* librettist, who stooped from the lofty heights of seventeenth-century Russian Realpolitik to supply a few generic poeticisms. Perhaps as a result of this division of labour, a stretch of the imagination is sometimes needed to span the gap between music and title: the sixth piece, 'In stormy times' ('Z bouřlivých dob'), for example, with its quotation from the scherzo of the Fourth Symphony, has rather more of *Walpurgisnacht* about it than the third one, 'Witches' sabbath' ('Noc filipojakubská'). Dvořák seems to have had a particular liking for the fifth piece, 'Silent woods' ('Klid'), which he arranged for cello and piano in 1891 (B.173) and for cello and orchestra in 1893 (B.182).

Dvořák left Prague for England on 5 March 1884. It was the longest trip he had ever undertaken, and he was nervous about it. He had never been to sea before, and had no more than a few words of phrasebook English. It is likely, too, that he was already suffering from the mysterious agoraphobic condition which afflicted him in later life. He certainly did not want to travel alone, and was therefore accompanied by a younger friend, the pianist Jindřich Kàan. As it turned out, the pair had an uneventful journey via Cologne and

Karel Bendl,
Antonín Dvořák,
Josef Bohuslav
Foerster, Jindřich
Kàan, Karel
Kovařovic, Zdeněk
Fibich, 1885

Brussels. The English Channel was like a boating lake, and they arrived at Dover on 8 March. There they were met by Ladislav Josef Zavertal, a recent acquaintance of Dvořák's who was military bandmaster with the Royal Artillery in Woolwich and was putting up Kàan for the duration of their stay. Zavertal shepherded them to Victoria Station, where they were welcomed by Alfred Littleton and the pianist Oscar Beringer, who would be Dvořák's host at his house in Hinde Street, off Manchester Square in Marylebone. The following day Dvořák's name was already all over the newspapers, Kàan noting (though how could he tell?) that some had had the diacritical marks specially cast for the occasion.

Dvořák was stunned by the scale and busyness of Victorian London. Neither Vienna nor Berlin had prepared him for the breathtaking grandeur of this hub of the British Empire, and he was equally amazed by the vastness of the venue, and the nearly one-thousand-strong choir and orchestra at his disposal, when he arrived at the Royal Albert Hall two days later to conduct choral rehearsals of the *Stabat mater*. The tone of open-mouthed wonder in which he relayed his impressions to friends back home is caught in a touchingly childlike letter to his widowed father in Kladno:

> *If all the* Czech inhabitants of the whole of Bohemia *were put together, they would not number as many as the inhabitants of London. And if all the inhabitants of the town of Kladno were to visit that enormous hall where I conducted my* Stabat mater, *there would still be plenty of room – for that is how huge the* Albert Hall is*!*

František had made it into the newspapers too, Antonín told him, as the butcher and innkeeper of Nelahozeves who had done everything he could to give his son a proper education;

and at the end of the letter he adds his own heartfelt thanks for that early support – another indication, if any were needed, that the traditional picture of son battling father to escape the clutches of the meat trade is more legend than fact. For his part, František continued to follow his son's English progress proudly in the newspapers, rejoicing in his successes and worrying about his safety on the transport network.

If five years earlier Dvořák had been overwhelmed to be fêted by the leading musicians of Austria and Germany, his reception in London was such as he could scarcely have imagined. Like Haydn almost a century before, he found himself lionised by musical and polite society. His first taste of what was in store came the evening after the Albert Hall rehearsal, when he turned up at Westwood House, Henry Littleton's palatial mansion in Sydenham, for what he thought was a small private dinner party but turned out to be a massive banquet in his honour. One hundred and fifty guests vied for his company, and an informal concert of his own music lasted into the early hours of the morning. Two days later, his *Stabat mater* concert at the Royal Albert Hall was greeted with ecstatic ovations from both audience and performers. And there was still a week to go before the Philharmonic Society concert he had actually come to London to give.

The Philharmonic Society was a far more go-ahead organisation than the tone of its correspondence might suggest. This was, after all, the body that had commissioned Beethoven's Ninth Symphony, as well as introducing to the public such fixtures of the modern concert hall as programme notes and the conductor's baton. It had fostered the careers of many composers and had brought to England some of the leading names in European music, including Spohr, Weber, Mendelssohn and Wagner. Seldom in its seventy-one-year history, though, had it seen an upsurge of popular enthusiasm such as followed Dvořák's concert at St James's Hall on 20 March. The Sixth Symphony, the second *Slavonic Rhapsody* and the *Hussite Overture* were cheered to the rafters, and 'Songs my mother taught me' – a number certain to appeal to the sentimental strain in Victorian taste – had to be encored. Two days later Dvořák conducted a concert that included the *Scherzo capriccioso* at that era-defining wonder of the modern world, the Crystal Palace. A couple of days after that he was the guest of honour at a huge Philharmonic Society banquet hosted at the Café Royal by the venerable composer Sir Julius Benedict, and after dinner he made a game stab at a few words of thanks in English. Journalists were as charmed by his unassuming manner as the critics were by his music. Even his famously undemonstrative style at the rostrum was praised for its honesty. London, one journal reported, was in the grip of something like 'Dvořák mania'.

All this adulation was an eye-opener for the composer. In later years grand receptions became an occupational hazard, and Dvořák at best a grudging lion, but there is no mistaking his enjoyment of this first taste of celebrity. His pleasure in it was more than personal, however. He was also alert to its significance for his country, writing home to his friend František Urbánek that he hoped his reception in England would not only mark the beginning of 'a happier time' for him but would 'bear Czech art in general good fruit'. Meanwhile, the music critic of *The Times*, Francis Hueffer, shrewdly gauged the creative opportunity presented to the composer himself by his London experiences. There was, he wrote, 'reason to expect that [Dvořák's] consciousness of addressing no longer a local circle of admirers but the musical world generally, will enlarge his views and strengthen his purposes'. He concluded presciently: 'it is probable, in short, that we have not yet heard the best of what Herr Dvořák has to say.'

For Dvořák himself, the last word on this triumphant first visit to a country he would come to love was a typical mixture of appreciation, fatalism and modesty. 'The English are a good, warm-hearted and music-loving nation,' he wrote in the same letter to Urbánek, 'and it is well known that when once they take a liking to someone, they remain faithful to him. God grant it may be so with me.' When he left London on 26 March he already knew he would be back soon. During the course of his stay he had agreed to conduct his *Stabat mater* again in September at the Three Choirs Festival in Worcester – or 'Worchester', as he wrote to his father – and had promised to compose a new symphony for the Philharmonic Society. He had also agreed to present at the 1885 Birmingham Musical Festival the as yet unwritten choral work commissioned by Novello, and to write an oratorio for the Leeds Music Festival in 1886. His first trip to England had thus generated at least three further ones.

Dvořák and Kàan arrived back in Prague on 29 March. The composer might have found a hero's welcome awaiting him at the station, had not plans for a grand reception fallen foul of the factionalism already polarising Czech musical opinion between Dvořák and Smetana – a polarity which would become dogmatised in twentieth-century Czechoslovakia. Dvořák is unlikely to have minded. He was probably looking at the engines anyway.

After a round of concert engagements in Plzeň, Olomouc and Prague, where he conducted *Dimitrij* at the National Theatre a week after stepping off the train, Dvořák withdrew to Vysoká to revise his *Hymnus* for publication by Novello; it appeared the following year, bearing the words 'dedicated with feelings of deep gratitude to the English people'. Only then was he free to start work on the cantata he had promised for Birmingham. This was *The Spectre's Bride* ('Svatební košile'), Op. 69 (B.135), his first major foray into what would be the characteristic territory of his final works: his country's supernatural folklore. It was while he was sketching the cantata that the Philharmonic Society wrote to inform him that he had been elected an honorary member; Dvořák replied in his inimitable broken English, thanking them for 'the rarely distinction.'

From May to August Dvořák worked on *The Spectre's Bride* in the converted granary on Count Kounic's estate where he and his family had spent their summers for the last four years. What part any continuing feelings for his sister-in-law may have played in his attachment to Vysoká must remain a matter of speculation; but he had certainly fallen in love with the place, and arrangements were already well in hand for making it a more permanent second home. He had a new piano sent down from Prague, and collected it by wagon from the nearby silver-mining town of Příbram. He had also bought an adjacent plot of land from his brother-in-law and was having a house built there on the foundations of an old sheepfold. Surrounded by a large garden planted with trees, the house was finished in October and became the family's regular summer home. (It is now known as the Villa Rusalka, after the title of his most famous opera.) Here he reclaimed the rural life of his childhood, getting up early to walk in the surrounding countryside, playing the organ in the local church, going to the pub with the neighbouring miners. He rejoiced in the sound of birdsong (insisting, however, that it never inspired him to music) and supplemented his unlikely urban hobby of trainspotting with the equally unlikely rural one of pigeon breeding. It was at Vysoká – a far cry from the pacey acclaim of his English tours – that, throughout the next two decades, he recharged his batteries in the intervals of an increasingly public life.

At the end of August Dvořák left behind the half-built house and the half-written cantata and set off once again for England. His travelling companion this time was the journalist and critic Václav Novotný, who later published his wide-eyed reminiscences of the trip. They arrived at Dover on 1 September and were met by Henry Littleton, who conveyed them to Westwood House, where they were to be his guests. It was there, sometime over the next few days, that Dvořák met the Brooklyn-based American composer Dudley Buck, who suggested the idea of a concert tour of the United States and offered to put Dvořák up. Nothing came of it at the time, but the conversation planted a seed in Dvořák's mind, and Novotný describes how, after greeting Buck's proposal very doubtfully, his friend suddenly seemed to warm to the idea.

After a few days of enjoying Littleton's lavish hospitality, Dvořák and Novotný travelled down to Worcester together. There, to his astonishment, the composer found his portrait for sale in all the bookshops, and was besieged by autograph-hunters in the street. On the morning of 11 September he conducted the *Stabat mater* in the cathedral, after which the local grandees Lord and Lady Compton held a breakfast reception for 300 people – an event that would no doubt have been even more gratifying had they not apparently forgotten to send an invitation to their guest of honour. That evening, when Dvořák conducted his Sixth Symphony, there were rousing ovations as he walked to the rostrum and thunderous applause after each of the movements. Novotný had never heard anything like it, and quickly revised his opinions of English reserve. Among the first violins was one young Englishman who described the electrifying effect of Dvořák's Slavic appearance 'among those placidly English faces' and drew an unforgettable pen-portrait of the composer, with his 'fierce peasant's jowl... striding down Foregate Street' and seeming 'as much out of place in Worcester as did his fervent Slavonic music when heard amongst the sedate hymn-tunes of the cantatas then being written for the festivals by English composers'. He was the twenty-seven-year-old Edward Elgar.

Five days later Dvořák was back at Vysoká, checking on the builders' progress, dashing off a *Dumka* and a *Furiant* for piano (Op. 12, B.135 & 136) and picking up the threads of *The Spectre's Bride*. Dvořák drew his text for the latter from Karel Jaromír Erben's *Garland of National Legends* ('Kytice z pověstí národních'), a collection of fantastical and often ghoulish ballads that would also provide the inspiration for four of his late symphonic poems. The cantata's Czech title translates as 'The Wedding Shift' (the more decorous English version was presumably a sop to Victorian sensibilities), and it recounts the legend of a girl whose absent lover returns and persuades her to accompany him on a long nocturnal journey. Their destination turns out to be a graveyard, the lover a corpse, and the prospective bride's wedding shift a winding sheet. In Dvořák's version the girl is saved from a fate indistinguishable from death by a fervent prayer to the Virgin. Set for three soloists, chorus and orchestra, *The Spectre's Bride* is divided into three parts – the girl's vigil and the arrival of her lover; the night journey; and the graveyard scene – which are bound together by repeated themes, including an ominous ticking motif first heard in the woodwinds in the opening section. There are several marvellous moments – the deep brass resonances of the graveyard scene; the grotesque folk march of the antepenultimate number (which infiltrates the memory like a virus); the girl's dignified aria of supplication to the Virgin – and Dvořák's way with the gothic suggests he could have made a fine living at the Hammer studios had he been born fifty years later. But in the end, the very structure of the folk-narrative, with its repeated episodes, militates against dramatic effectiveness in the concert hall. Dvořák himself was tremendously excited by the cantata, telling Göbl it was the best thing he had ever written. Posterity has been more equivocal, however, and the work is rarely heard today.

By the time he put the finishing touches to the cantata in November, Dvořák's experiences in England must have seemed to him, as they did to Novotný, like 'a marvellous and beautiful dream'. But if events north of the Channel had opened an exciting new musical front to him, they had in some ways complicated matters closer to home. In particular, they had introduced an element of friction into his relationship with his principal publisher. Simrock had taken umbrage at Dvořák's inclusion of the as yet unpublished *Hussite Overture* in his London programme in March, and tried unsuccessfully to make him withdraw it. He also objected to the untidiness of some of the manuscripts Dvořák was sending him for publication. Such disputes, petty in themselves and perhaps inevitable in such a close professional partnership, reflected at root a shift in the balance of power between composer and publisher. Dvořák had always found other outlets for works Simrock was uninterested in (or, for that matter, works he did not want Simrock to have). Likewise, he had always known how to haggle over terms. But with Novello's appearance on the scene, and buoyed by the newly discovered fervour of English demand for his work, he suddenly found himself in a very much stronger negotiating position. He now had another estimate to set against Simrock's, both commercially and aesthetically, and one, moreover, beyond the reach of the political and ethnic tensions that distorted the central European musical marketplace.

Those tensions were still very much on his mind in 1884. In the summer Hanslick had renewed his exhortations to Dvořák to write a German opera for German audiences, but while the composer seemed airily enough inclined to accept in one of his letters to Simrock, he still significantly held off from taking the bait. England had not only strengthened his hand, it had, as Hueffer had predicted in *The Times*, also broadened his horizons. And just as it introduced him to an audience whose appreciation of his Czechness was uncontaminated by the politics of the Habsburg Monarchy, so it made possible a kind of internationalism which neither demanded the surrender of his national identity nor valued it only for its exoticism. There is a new assertiveness to his correspondence with Simrock as he restates his wish that the titles of his works should appear in both Czech and German, and his Christian name as the neutral 'Ant.' rather than the German 'Anton'. The letters reach a climax of irritation in 1885 when Simrock seems unable to treat his requests with the seriousness they deserve: 'Do not laugh at my Czech brothers,' Dvořák snapped in August that year, 'and do not be sorry for me either... It is evident that you have no idea of the circumstances in which I live.' The following month, in response to another uncomprehending letter from Simrock, he reasserted his patriotism in a frequently quoted passage:

Your last letter with national-political comments I found very entertaining; I only regret that you are so badly informed... But what have we two to do with politics; let us be glad that we can dedicate our services to art. And let us hope that nations which possess and represent art will never perish, no matter how small they are. Forgive me but I only wanted to say to you that an artist has also his country in which he must have firm faith and for which he must have an ardent heart.

The tone is conciliatory, but it is also that of a man who can afford to conciliate because he knows where he stands, and the ground is firm under his feet. Vienna never got its German opera.

Soon after he completed *The Spectre's Bride* at the end of November 1884, Dvořák began sketching the symphony he had promised to write for the Philharmonic Society. Universally regarded as among his very greatest works, the Symphony No. 7 in D minor, Op. 70 (B.141) has also been seen as the crucial stage in the resolution of these crises of conscience and loyalty. Whatever its psychological wellsprings, the symphony represents an order of achievement which only the F minor Piano Trio had approached before, and like the trio it was the product of much evolutionary struggle in the composer's sketchbooks. Dvořák told his friend Antonín Rus that he wanted the new work to shake the world, and the tragic intensity of its language is unprecedented in his output. There are few parallels in the symphonic literature for the atmosphere of dark foreboding with which the opening *Allegro maestoso* begins. Tragedy is seldom far from the surface in the inner movements either, breaking through in the stormy episodes of the exquisite *Poco adagio* and even darkening the closing pages of the scherzo. It is also the keynote of the finale, the D major of whose concluding *tierces de Picardie* sounds like a willed gesture of defiance in the face of the inevitable.

Dvořák finished the Seventh Symphony on 17 March 1885, and a few days later conducted the premiere of *The Spectre's Bride* in Plzeň. On 19 April he and his inevitable travelling companion, now the Czech linguist Josef Zubatý, arrived in England for the first of two visits in 1885. On 22 April he conducted the first performance of the symphony at the Philharmonic Society concert in St James's Hall. The concert was a great success and the work's unfamiliar idiom made a profound, if mixed, impression on both audience and critics. As well as giving the premiere of the symphony, he also conducted his Piano Concerto with Franz Rummel as soloist at a Philharmonic Society concert on 6 May, and a performance of the newly revised *Hymnus* a week later. The former was even better received than the symphony.

At four weeks, Dvořák's third visit to England was his longest yet, and between social occasions, which included a dinner of the Royal Society of Musicians at which he was guest of honour, he was able to sample the London tourist trail, walking in Hyde Park and Regent's Park, visiting the National Gallery (where he likened the Raphael Madonna to the music of Mozart) and going to the theatre. As on his previous visit, he stayed with the Littletons, noting with his gardener's eye that the roses in the grounds of Westwood House bloomed a whole month earlier than at Vysoká.

Later that year, the Dvořáks spent their first summer in their new house at Vysoká. Dvořák devoted his time to unwinding after the concentrated creative effort of the Seventh Symphony, and the only new work to emerge during that period was the short *Hymn of the Czech Peasants* ('Hymna českého rolnictva') for mixed choir and orchestra, Op. 28 (B.143). It was also during this summer of 1885 that his relations with Simrock went through their rockiest phase so far. Added to the stand-off over the publishing of his works in both Czech and German was the fact that Dvořák was asking 6,000 marks for his new symphony, whereas Simrock was only prepared to offer 3,000 – a fifth of what he paid for a Brahms symphony. Whether or not it was a bluff, Dvořák claimed to have been offered the higher sum by another publisher and stood his ground. There was a tense meeting between the two men at Karlovy Vary (Carlsbad) and a deal was eventually hammered out, Dvořák agreeing to throw in a new set of Slavonic dances for the money he was demanding. It left a sour taste in the mouth, though, and relations remained fraught for some time.

Dvořák set off for England again on 15 August, travelling alone for the first time. He seems to have made some eccentric timetabling choices, crossing the Channel at night, arriving in London at six o'clock in the morning to find the streets silent and deserted, and travelling straight up to Birmingham the same afternoon for a choral rehearsal of *The Spectre's Bride* in the evening. The following day he had to shuttle back down to London to rehearse the instrumentalists, there being no resident orchestra in Birmingham. He must have needed the short break he then took in Brighton, where Littleton had a house. The bustle and paraphernalia of this well-to-do Victorian seaside resort astonished him: the ladies, he reported, even did their sea bathing in public!

Not at first sight calculated to appeal to the citizens of a Midlands industrial town, Dvořák's lurid central European ghost story in fact catered toothsomely to the Victorian appetite for high melodrama, and even by the standards of his previous English tours his concert on the 27 August was a sensational success. The reaction was near-hysterical. Audience and performers crowded round him, chanting his name and jostling each other for a chance to shake his hand. The critics declared him a 'magician', and *The Spectre's Bride* was launched on a quite extraordinary circuit of performances that rippled out through the Anglophone world from London and the provinces to the American Mid-West, Canada and even Australia.

While Dvořák was in Birmingham he had a meeting with the octogenarian Cardinal Newman, who gave the visitor a copy of his spiritual epic *The Dream of Gerontius*. But Dvořák already had a subject in mind for his next choral work, the one he had promised to write for the following year's Leeds Music Festival. Newman's poem would not be set for another fifteen years, and the composer then was not Dvořák but

Elgar, who had once again witnessed the adoration of the Czech composer from his desk in the first violins.

Dvořák left England the day after the performance and was home again by the end of August. A few days later (the very same day that he wrote his affirmation of patriotism to Simrock) he sent a charming thank-you letter to Littleton, written in his best English:

> *The verry merry days of Birmingham ar over and naw stay I agin quiet alone as before. Daily I am walking in the beutyful forestes and reflecting about Ludmila.*

Ludmila, a ninth-century saint and a key figure in the conversion of Bohemia to Christianity, was to be the subject of Dvořák's oratorio for Leeds, *Saint Ludmila* ('Svatá Ludmila'), Op. 71 (B.144). Any doubts Littleton and others had had about how well such a recondite subject would go down in municipal Yorkshire seem to have been dispelled by the spectacular reception of *The Spectre's Bride* in Birmingham; and a week after writing his letters to Littleton and Simrock, Dvořák made a start on the new work, using a libretto specially prepared for him by the Czech poet Jaroslav Vrchlický. *Saint Ludmila*, like *The Spectre's Bride*, is in three parts, and by November Dvořák had finished the sketch of Part One. The manuscript bears the cryptic inscription, 'Finished during the time when *The Cunning Peasant* was murdered in Vienna' – a reference to the catastrophic performance of his opera there a few days earlier, when anti-Czech sentiment was running high in the city and students were demonstrating in the streets. If he needed any further confirmation that he had been right not to sell his operatic soul for Austria, it came within days, when *Dimitrij* was performed to great acclaim in a revised version at the National Theatre in Prague.

Whereas *The Spectre's Bride* had fairly flowed from his pen, *Saint Ludmila* caused Dvořák enormous difficulty. The score occupied him to the exclusion of almost everything else from September 1885 to the end of May 1886, and to judge by his letters to friends it brought him at times to the edge of despair. It is little wonder, then, that his patience sounds close to breaking point in letters to Simrock during this period. The publisher was pressing him for the second set of Slavonic dances for piano duet that he had undertaken to write as part of their publication deal for the Seventh Symphony, but Dvořák was hardly in the mood for what he called 'such light music', still less to revisit his manner of eight years ago: 'I must inform you,' he wrote in January 1886, 'that it will not by any means be such a simple matter with the Slavonic Dances as it was the first time. To do the same thing twice over is damnably difficult.' (Did that last phrase perhaps have as much to do with *The Spectre's Bride* and *Saint Ludmila* as with the *Slavonic Dances*? After all, with each of his triumphs in England the bar of expectation was raised a little higher.) Letters flew irritably backwards and forwards. Simrock added to his list of complaints the claim that Dvořák should have given him first option on *Saint Ludmila* before selling it to Novello (for £650, with provision for an extra £350 if it was a success), and invoked their contractual arrangements of 1877. Dvořák, who was apt to run the gamut of negotiating ploys with little regard for consistency, pleaded the financial needs of his growing family. (He now had five children: in addition to Otilie, Anna and Magda, there were two more sons. Antonín had been born in March 1883, and Otakar – whom with singular lack of superstition they named after their lost firstborn – was born in February 1885. The family would be completed by the birth of Aloisie, known as Zinda, in April 1888.) But there was no doubt who had the upper hand these days. At one point, with lordly *élan*, Dvořák even replied to Simrock's protestations in English.

There is a marked change of tone, however, as soon as *Saint Ludmila* is safely out of the way. In June Dvořák broke the ice with a breezy letter telling Simrock how beautiful the weather and the countryside were at Vysoká, where, he said, he was already well underway with the *Slavonic Dances* and aiming to finish them the following month. He was as good as his word, and by 9 July the piano duet versions were done and dusted (B.145). His only other new composition of the summer was a set of four songs on folk poems for voice and piano, *In Folk Tone* ('V národním tónu'), Op. 73 (B.146), a bouquet of art-songs to Czech and Slovak folk texts that Simrock, with his customary insensitivity to the patriotic feelings of his Bohemian client, published in German translation under the title *Im Volkston*.

Dvořák made just one trip to England in 1886, and this time he took his wife with him. The couple left Prague on 1 October, and two days later Anna was introduced to the prosperous ways of the Littletons at Westwood House. On 15 October Dvořák conducted the premiere of *Saint Ludmila* at the Leeds Music Festival, and it was received with cheers, applause and waving of handkerchiefs, albeit without the wildly adulatory scenes that had greeted *The Spectre's Bride* in Birmingham the previous year. Like the cantata, *Saint Ludmila* has been a casualty of changing tastes; in this case, however, the change seems perceptibly to have begun even during Dvořák's stay in England. There was a certain amount of critical foot-shuffling about the sheer length of the work – with intervals, it lasted three-and-a-half hours – and the composer made cuts for two further performances in London, the second of which, at the Crystal Palace on 6 November, was poorly attended. Most significantly, whereas the Birmingham premiere of *The*

Dvořák and his wife in London, 1886

Spectre's Bride was the catalyst for choral societies all over the world to include the work in their programmes, future performances of *Saint Ludmila* remained thin on the ground, especially outside the Czech lands. Novello never had to pay that additional £350.

After five visits in two-and-a-half years, Dvořák had inevitably lost something of his novelty value in England, though clearly none of the respect in which he was held as a composer. Whether or not for this reason, he decided, after arriving back in Bohemia in early November 1886, to make a break with the pattern that had defined his working life since March 1884 (an English visit followed by a new composition in preparation for his next English visit), and apart from some conducting engagements in European cities, plus a significant Russian tour in March 1890, he spent most of the next three-and-a-half years at home.

His first task was already awaiting him when he got back. Having received the piano duet versions of the *Slavonic Dances*, Simrock was now pressing him for orchestrations, albeit in a tone of comradely banter which suggests that, for the time being at least, relations were back on an even keel. Dvořák always liked to present orchestration as journeyman work that any jobbing musician could do as well as he, and he had certainly been dragging his heels over orchestrating the dances. There is, however, not the slightest sign of that reluctance in the finished versions, which he produced on his return from England and completed early in the New Year. On the contrary, Dvořák's mastery of the orchestral palette appears so fresh, and the scoring so inevitable, that – unlike the *Legends* – the original piano duets seem monochrome by comparison.

Many critics regard Dvořák's second set of eight *Slavonic Dances*, Op. 72 (B.147), as a finer work even than his first, but it has never quite matched the Op. 46 set in wider popularity. One can only marvel, though, at the undiminished vitality of Dvořák's imagination after the arduous succession of compositions for England that had occupied him for so long. The dances are by no means a raking over of old coals: as is clear from his letters to Simrock, Dvořák had the artist's horror of self-repetition and he consciously set out to produce something different this time. The first and penultimate dances are uninhibited romps, but there is also an underlying thoughtfulness to this set, felt for example in the second, fourth and final dances, which contrasts with the more consistently extrovert Op. 46. The Op. 72 set also ranges more widely than the first, some of the dances looking as far afield as Poland and the Balkans, and it has provoked the same degree of debate about sources and influences. As with Op. 46, however, what impresses itself on the listener is the apparently effortless way in which Dvořák assimilates folk idioms to his own musical language, while losing nothing of their spontaneity of spirit.

As soon as he had despatched the *Slavonic Dances*, which are sometimes seen as ushering in a second 'Slavonic period' in Dvořák's work, he embarked on the hectic programme of composition that was to occupy him almost uninterruptedly until his return to England in the spring of 1890. During this period he not only produced original works in a great variety of genres (including chamber music, sacred choral music, keyboard works, songs, a symphony and an opera), he also undertook intensive revision of several earlier works, not least to meet the growing demand from Simrock and other publishers for 'unknown' Dvořák. These included the Second, Third, Fourth and Fifth symphonies, the String Quartet No. 8 in E major, the String Quintet in G major, and the *Symphonic Variations*. This last work, which Dvořák unearthed and conducted in Prague in March 1887, was the occasion of Richter's triumph when he presented it at one of his London concerts in May. (It was equally successful in Vienna later in the year: Brahms was so taken with it that he presented Dvořák with a cigar-holder as a mark of his esteem.)

A mere two days after finishing the orchestration of the *Slavonic Dances* he sat down to compose a work that, after all the grand public stages of his recent experience, returned him to the more intimate arena of home music making. This, the *Terzetto* for two violins and viola, Op. 74 (B.148) was in fact home music making in the most literal sense since it was written for a fellow-resident of Dvořák's own house, a chemistry student called Josef Kruis, and his violin teacher Jan Pelikán. Like the *Bagatelles* he had written for Srb-Debrnov, the *Terzetto* seems to revel in the limitations and challenges imposed by the unusual combination of instruments available to the performers (the viola player being Dvořák himself). The result is a self-contained work of great charm and deceptive simplicity. The *Larghetto* second movement is a beautifully transparent cavatina, and the finale a set of variations on a many-jointed theme, the potential of which, like that of the *Symphonic Variations*, lies in its ambiguities. Unfortunately, Kruis proved unequal to the demands of the *Terzetto*'s first violin part, so Dvořák proceeded to write another, easier work for the same combination of instruments: the four *Miniatures* ('Drobnosti'), Op. 75a (B.149). He then immediately arranged this new work for violin and piano, in which form it was published as *Romantic Pieces* ('Romantické kusy'), Op. 75 (B.150), and is more usually heard today. In all three works, which occupied Dvořák for less than three weeks in January 1887, there is the sense of a master relaxing in everything but commitment to his craft. He told Simrock that he enjoyed writing these bagatelles as much as a symphony, and it shows.

Dvořák's next original composition of 1887 is a very different piece, but one which, perhaps unexpectedly, has something of the same sense of informality as the miniatures written for Kruis. The Mass in D major, Op. 86 (B.153), is a short setting for four soloists, mixed choir and organ. Commissioned by Josef Hlávka – the founding president of the Czech Academy of Sciences and Arts – for the consecration of his private chapel at Lužany Castle, it too was a family affair: at the consecration ceremony the two female parts were sung by Hlávka's wife, Zdeňka, and Anna Dvořáková – a reminder that the composer's wife was a well-respected contralto in her own right. As the intimate setting of the chapel might suggest, the Mass is an unpretentious expression of faith, predominantly contented in tone, with the solo organ providing sufficient astringency to avoid cloyingness. There is a real sense of holy mystery in the 'Incarnatus est' and the peaceful 'Benedictus'; while, in keeping with the tone of the whole work, the concluding 'Agnus Dei', with its calm fugal opening, is expressive more of confident gratitude than of soul-searching guilt. Dvořák later produced a more public version of the Mass, scored for orchestra instead of organ (B.175), which was published by Novello and first performed at the Crystal Palace by August Manns in 1893.

Among the works Dvořák revised in 1887 were two from his earliest years as a composer: the String Quartet No. 1 in A major and the much-revisited song cycle *Cypresses*. In the latter case he produced an arrangement for string quartet (B.152) of twelve of the original songs under the wonderfully evocative title *Echo of Songs* ('Ohlas písní'), later changed to *Evening Songs* ('Večerní písně') but generally known today by the title of the original song cycle. If the sequence wears its heart too unstintingly on its sleeve to work as a single concert piece, each of its individual numbers is nonetheless a powerful evocation of remembered love.

Another of the 'old sins' Dvořák revisited in 1887 was the Piano Quintet in A major from 1872 (B.28), one of his first chamber works to be heard by the Prague public. Here he was less successful in marrying to his satisfaction the spirit of youth and the craftsmanship of maturity and, as on previous occasions when a composition fell short of his ambitions, he decided to start again from scratch: between 18 August and 3 October he produced a new piano quintet in the same key, creating in the process one of his finest and best-known chamber works. Drawing attention to the breadth of its emotional spectrum, John Clapham wrote of the Piano Quintet in A major, Op. 81 (B.155), that it 'probably epitomizes more completely the genuine Dvořák style in most of its facets than any other work of his'. The slow movement, much admired by Tchaikovsky, is a sustainedly elegiac *dumka*, but there are intimations of loss below the surface cheer of the opening movement too, and a sense of *lacrimae rerum* permeates even the more carefree scherzo and finale.

By the autumn of 1887 five years had elapsed since the composition of *Dimitrij*, the longest period Dvořák had ever allowed to pass without an opera on the stocks (though during the early months of 1887 he had revised the final act of *King and Charcoal Burner* for a performance at the National Theatre in June (B.151)). He had, however, been considering subjects for a new opera almost continuously since *Dimitrij* – including, of course, some proffered by the Vienna Court Opera – and had gone so far as to commission a comic libretto from his *Dimitrij* collaborator Marie Červinková-Riegrová, only to put it into cold storage for years when he received it. This was *The Jacobin*, the story of a young nobleman (Bohuš) who returns incognito to Bohemia after living in

117

Paris during the Revolution to find that his father, Count Vilém, has disinherited him for his supposed Jacobinism. The main plot concerns the trials of Bohuš, who is imprisoned, unrecognised, by the Count, and of his young wife Julie, who persuades Vilém to release and reinstate her husband by a benign subterfuge. The emotional focus of the work, however, is the village schoolteacher-cum-choirmaster Benda and his daughter Terinka. Benda is clearly modelled on Dvořák's old Zlonice mentor Antonín Liehmann (whose own daughter was called Terinka) and the opera is in large part a tribute to the Bohemian tradition of community music making to which Liehmann belonged and which served Dvořák himself so well in his formative years. Benda is seen rehearsing his village choir, admitting the 'stranger' Bohuš to his house on the grounds that no one who loves music can be untrustworthy, helping Julie convert the Count, and finally letting Terinka marry the man she loves rather than the man he has chosen for her. Considering how closely this story maps the settings and sympathies of Dvořák's early years, it is perhaps surprising that it took him so long to decide to set it, though he clearly remained doubtful about how well it would travel outside Bohemia. He only made up his mind in summer 1887 when Červinková finally lost patience with his procrastination and asked him to send the libretto back to her if he wasn't going to use it. He started work on 10 November and for the whole of the next year devoted himself to the opera, completing it on 18 November 1888.

The Jacobin ('Jakobín'), Op. 84 (B.159) is perhaps the most characteristic of Dvořák's operatic achievements up to this point. The life of the village – surely Nelahozeves in all but name – is lovingly evoked from the very first bars of Act I, and the long scene at the beginning of Act II in which Benda rehearses the children's choir is as effective as it is imbued with nostalgic affection: there is, in particular, a wonderful innocence to the music Dvořák gives the choir, which forms a kind of backdrop to the entire action. There are two surgingly romantic duets, at once radiant and troubled, for Terinka and Jiří in Acts I and II. Most moving of all, though, is the climactic scene in Act III in which Julie, singing offstage the lullaby Bohuš's mother used to sing, revives the Count's memories of his 'lost' son's babyhood and causes him to realise the continuing depth of his paternal love. It is a moment of quiet drama in which the redemptive power of music is simply and powerfully enacted, and it is hard not to feel behind it the resonance of the Dvořáks' own family losses of the 1870s. *The Jacobin* is a cornerstone of what has been called Dvořák's second national period; but while the opera is proudly and rootedly Bohemian, the spirit of its nationalism is perhaps best encapsulated in Julie's rhetorical question, 'Jsme z Čech – / a vy se pte, / zda snéme pět?': 'We're Czechs – / and you ask us / if we can sing?' 'This time,' Dvořák wrote to Göbl, 'I believe that those who have doubts about my *dramatic talent* will be satisfied, if not surprised.' The reception of *The Jacobin* at the National Theatre in Prague when it was first performed on 12 February 1889 fully justified his belief; but equally justified, as it turned out, were his fears that the opera's provincial setting would limit its appeal outside the Czech lands.

On 12 February 1888, a year to the day before the *Jacobin* premiere, Dvořák had attended a performance of Verdi's *Otello* at the National Theatre. There, in the interval, Marie Červinková's father, the leading politician František Ladislav Rieger, introduced him to a visiting musical celebrity who had arrived in Prague for the first time the previous day. Pyotr Il'yich Tchaikovsky was then forty-seven, a little over a year older than Dvořák himself, and was halfway through a three-month European tour that had already taken in Berlin, Leipzig

Pyotr Il'yich Tchaikovsky in 1888

and Hamburg and would continue to Paris and London. Like Dvořák's visits to England, this tour was the composer's first real exposure to a broad audience outside his homeland and opened his eyes to the extent of his reputation in the wider world. The centre of attention wherever he went, he had been introduced to Brahms, Grieg, Mahler and Busoni and had attended his share of musical and civic receptions. Nowhere, however, was he greeted with such unrestrained, indeed almost frenzied, adulation as in Prague, where he was seen not only as a musician of international standing but as a roving ambassador for Slavic culture and a living symbol of pan-Slavic pride. He and Dvořák hit it off immediately, and for the remainder of Tchaikovsky's stay in the city the two men spent part of every day in each other's company. Tchaikovsky heard and loved Dvořák's Piano Quintet, Op. 81, and Dvořák made him a gift of the printed score of the Seventh Symphony and the piano reduction of *Dimitrij*. He came to lunch at Dvořák's flat, where they talked about Slavic music (ironically in German, their only shared language), and was clearly charmed by Dvořák's personal eccentricities, describing him in a letter to a friend as 'the dear funny fellow'. But he was also a sincere admirer of Dvořák's music, for which he became a committed evangelist back in Russia. When Tchaikovsky returned to Prague in the autumn to conduct his Fifth Symphony and his opera *Eugene Onegin* he brought with him an invitation from the Imperial Russian Music Society, asking Dvořák to conduct a programme of

Czech music in Moscow. (Always reluctant to travel alone, Dvořák made reflexive excuses, but eventually agreed to schedule a visit for March 1890.) Once again, Tchaikovsky saw Dvořák every day, and Dvořák attended every rehearsal of *Eugene Onegin*.

Shortly after finishing *The Jacobin* at the end of 1888 Dvořák made yet another raid on his *Cypresses* song cycle for the eight *Love Songs* ('Písně milostné') for voice and piano, Op. 83 (B.160), the pervasive yearning of which is perhaps most beautifully expressed in the second and seventh songs, 'Never will love lead us' ('Ó, naší lasce nekvete') and 'When thy sweet glances on me fall' ('V té sladké moci očí tvých'). There then ensued one of the longest periods of creative inactivity in Dvořák's life to date. For almost four months, perhaps because of ill health, he wrote nothing at all. Only in mid-April did he take up his pen again, to compose the thirteen *Poetic Tone Pictures* ('Poetické nálady') for piano, Op. 85 (B.161), a heterogeneous collection of miniatures with colourful titles (for which this time he seems not to have had to call on Červinková) such as 'At the old castle' ('Na starém hradě'), 'Goblins' dance' ('Rej skřítků') and 'Bacchanalia'. The eleventh piece, 'Tittle-tattle' ('Na táčkách'), is the only one to contradict Dvořák's assurance to Simrock that, despite the titles, the *Pictures* 'don't sound Schumannesque', but the sixth piece, 'Reverie' ('Vzpomínání'), sounds so extraordinarily *Chopin*esque that it must surely be intended as a homage to the Polish composer. Dvořák described the *Poetic Tone Pictures* as 'in a way programme music', and they therefore represent a small but significant step across what in the musical world of the second half of the nineteenth century was an ideological as well as a stylistic boundary. Artificially rigid as such distinctions now appear, not least due to Dvořák himself, for contemporary critics whose taste ran to partisanship 'programme music' was the province of Liszt and Wagner. They considered it antithetical to 'absolute music', the province of Brahms and his followers, where Dvořák, despite his lifelong admiration of Wagner, had been seen to belong. Unassuming as they are, the *Poetic Tone Pictures* thus point ahead to Dvořák's openly programmatic music of the following decade. They are also a mark of that aesthetic open-mindedness which characterised him throughout his career (and which would prove in short supply among critics wrong-footed by his new musical direction in the 1890s).

Dvořák told Simrock that he had taken great pains over the *Poetic Tone Pictures*; certainly in the past he had written entire symphonies in less than the seven weeks it took to complete them. There was no return of the silence that had preceded them, however. The following month, at Vysoká, he started work on his Piano Quartet in E flat major, Op. 87 (B.162) (another work that Simrock had been urging him to compose) and finished it a little over a month later, in the middle of August 1889. Like his only previous essay in the form, the Piano Quartet in D major from 1875, the Piano Quartet in E flat is one of Dvořák's less performed chamber works. It is, however, a far more substantial piece than its predecessor and would occupy a more conspicuous place in his chamber output but for the unqualified success of the Piano Quintet in A major from two years earlier. Dvořák told Göbl, one of few correspondents whom he admitted to the everyday trials and pleasures of his composing life, that the melodies for this work fairly surged upon him, and in the slow movement in particular there is an extraordinary abundance of thematic material. The delightful scherzo has a loping waltz-like main subject and a mysteriously oriental-sounding secondary theme, and the piano seems at times to be metamorphosing into a cimbalom. The finale, a restless display of Slavonic energy, barely pauses for breath.

No sooner had Dvořák finished the Piano Quartet than he started work on his Symphony No. 8 in G major, Op. 88 (B.163). Just as the Seventh Symphony sets out to be something altogether different from his Sixth, so the Eighth could hardly be further in tone from its austerely tragic predecessor. A genial and relatively loosely structured work, it has nonetheless proved the most controversial of Dvořák's mature symphonies, polarising critical opinion between those who see it as the most unconstrainedly natural of his symphonic inspirations and those who only grudgingly accord it symphonic status at all. The free variation-form finale in particular has seemed to some to fall short of Dvořák's usual symphonic standards. But the Eighth Symphony is Dvořák in holiday shirtsleeves, enjoying the birdsong and sunshine of Vysoká, and it is hard not to be disarmed by the openness of his greeting and the sheer rhapsodic profusion of his melody.

The symphony occupied Dvořák from August to November 1889. Some time during the writing of it he decided not to accept a tempting post he had been offered earlier in the year as professor of composition and instrumentation at the Prague Conservatoire, which was gearing up for amalgamation with his *alma mater*, the Prague Organ School. The Czech music critic Ladislav Dolanský remembered bumping into Dvořák at Urbánek's music shop during this time, and Dvořák making it gruffly clear to the customers that he wasn't cut out for teaching: 'My duty is to write, do you understand, and not to teach,' Dolanský recalled him saying. 'I am too much of an old bear, and nobody will get me into doing that.' Accordingly he rejected the Conservatoire's offer, claiming that pressure of composition and travel would prevent him from fulfilling all his duties – a patent, if diplomatic, inversion of his true concern.

In October he took a break from work on the symphony to go to Berlin, where Hans von Bülow conducted his Seventh Symphony two days in a row towards the end of the month. Bülow, to whom Dvořák had retrospectively dedicated his Fifth Symphony two years earlier, gave a magnificent account of the work, and the composer was so delighted that in a fit of schoolboyish enthusiasm he pasted the conductor's photograph onto the title page of his autograph score.

In June an official seal had been put on Dvořák's reputation in the German-speaking world when he was awarded the prestigious Order of the Iron Crown, third class, by the Emperor; and in December he and Anna travelled to Vienna to be received in audience by Franz Josef himself, together with Brahms, who had been made Commander of the Order of Leopold for his services to music. Bohemia was quick to match imperial recognition with honour for the prophet in his own country, and in February 1890 the Prague Artistic Society held a banquet for Dvořák. Shortly afterwards he was awarded an honorary doctorate at the Czech University of Prague and elected to the Czech Academy of Sciences and Arts.

With the dawn of the New Year, however, Dvořák's thoughts were turning once again to England. Ever since the success of *The Spectre's Bride* there in 1885, the organisers of the Birmingham Festival had been trying to persuade him to favour them with another major choral work. He had held off from committing himself to the next in their three-yearly cycle of festivals, in 1888, but at the beginning of 1890 he got in touch with the organising committee to say that he would be prepared to write a Requiem for the 1891 event. A Catholic Mass for the dead was not perhaps the most obvious follow-up to *The Spectre's Bride*, but the committee was gratified by the offer, and Dvořák began work on the *Requiem* straightaway. For the next ten months no other compositions were allowed to intrude on its creation – apart from a short *Gavotte* for three violins (B.164), written one August day at Vysoká for a beginner's book of violin pieces. But there were plenty of other interruptions, beginning with the premiere of the Eighth Symphony, which Dvořák himself conducted in Prague on 2 February. Then, at the end of the month, he and Anna set off for Russia.

Dvořák's Russian visit was a curiously low-key affair. At the personal level he was disappointed to find that Tchaikovsky was out of the country for the duration of his stay, while publicly there was none of the spontaneous outpouring of pan-Slavic pride that had characterised Tchaikovsky's visit to Prague two years earlier. Even the official welcome was muted, particularly in Moscow where formal tokens of respect such as were becoming routine for him elsewhere in Europe were largely restricted to the expatriate Czech and German communities. To make matters worse, illness forced last-minute changes to the line-up for his concert in Moscow on 11 March. Dvořák, who suspected he had been the victim of intrigue, reported back to a friend in Vienna that while it had gone well it had not gone as well as he had expected, and unburdened himself of some sardonic observations on 'Slavonic brotherhood'. Eleven days later he conducted at a second concert, this time in St Petersburg, and here his own contributions, the Sixth Symphony and the *Scherzo capriccioso*, were much more enthusiastically received. Afterwards a dinner was held in his honour at the Evropa Hotel, and he was toasted by the influential president of the Russian Musical Society and founder of the St Petersburg Conservatoire Anton Rubinstein. The next day the Dvořáks left Russia for Prague.

Matters were very different the following month when

Dvořák returned to England for a short visit, his first since 1887. The English premiere of his Eighth Symphony, at a Philharmonic Society Concert in St James's Hall on 24 April, was greeted with the customary ovations. As with his earlier English triumphs, however, the trip brought difficulties in its wake. Relations between Simrock and the composer were again going through one of their difficult patches, and the publisher's lack of interest in the Eighth Symphony (which Dvořák was confident of being able to sell to Novello if he could not get the price he wanted from Simrock) sent them into a downward spiral of recrimination. All the old arguments resurfaced: Dvořák threatened no longer to offer Simrock first refusal on large-scale works, Simrock threatened legal action in return, and in October the composer broke off communications entirely. He then proceeded to negotiate a deal with Novello on the symphony, the *Requiem* and the orchestrated version of his Mass. It was the most serious rupture so far, and not until 1893 were relations properly restored.

Dvořák completed the score of the *Requiem*, Op. 89 (B.165) on 31 October 1890. The following month he received a letter from that pillar of the Victorian musical establishment Charles Villiers Stanford, asking whether he would be prepared to receive an honorary doctorate from the University of Cambridge, where Stanford himself was Professor of Music. For Dvořák the question was virtually rhetorical – 'it goes without saying,' he wrote to Gobl, 'that I shall accept it' – and arrangements were made for him to attend a degree ceremony the following summer.

It was in November too that he began work on one of his most celebrated chamber works, the *Dumky* piano trio, Op. 90 (B.166). The trio is organised on entirely original lines, being a succession of six movements, each in the form of a *dumka*, the first three of which are played without a break. As with all Dvořák's characteristic *dumky* (Czech plural of *dumka*), the music is melancholy with lively interludes, the alternation of moods here being elevated to the organising principle of the entire work. The composer himself gave the first performance, together with his friends Ferdinand Lachner and Hanuš Wihan, at a concert held in April 1891 to celebrate his honorary doctorate at the Czech University; and together with 'The American' Quartet and the Piano Quintet, Op. 81, the *Dumky* trio has remained one of his most popular chamber works.

Around the same time that Dvořák started work on the *Dumky* trio, the Prague Conservatoire, not to be put off by his rejection of their initial approach, renewed their offer of a professorship. Their persistence paid dividends: despite the fact that there had been no material change in his circumstances since the previous year, this time Dvořák accepted the post. The decision made an enormous difference to his life. He was now an employee for the first time since giving up his post as organist at St Adalbert's in 1877, and for more than a decade from January 1891, when he took up his duties at the Conservatoire, teaching would provide the framework for all his professional activities. If the move represented a loss of freedom in one direction, however, it was soon to open up an unprecedented opportunity in another, since without it he might never have been invited to teach in the United States.

Dvořák's teaching methods were, to say the least, unorthodox. As his own examiners' report from the Prague Organ School had observed so many years before, his natural inclination was towards the practical rather than the theoretical. He set great store by compositional experience, requiring a new piece of writing from his students at every class (and there were three a week), but he was an instinctual critic and often inarticulate in his reactions. He was prepared to teach only the most talented students, from whom he demanded rigorous independent thought. Anyone could have a good idea, he said, but it was the working out of the idea that mattered: composition was the ability 'to make a great deal – a very great deal – out of nothing much'. His bearing and judgement were (by modern standards highly unprofessionally) subject to his volatile moods, and he was capable not only of humiliating brusqueness but also of demoralising inconsistency. He could, for example, be enthusiastic about parts of a composition at one class, only to disparage precisely the same parts at the following one; and one pupil recalled rewriting a passage because Dvořák had said it was too simple, only to be told at the next session that it would be much more effective if it were simpler. Students were staggered by his compendious knowledge of the great masters, whole passages of whose work he could play from memory, and they knew he would pounce on any hint of derivativeness. At the same time, his valuations could be cryptic to the point of obscurity, and his idiosyncrasies of expression sometimes more memorable than enlightening. In one famous instance, he demanded to know 'What is Mozart?' and became increasingly frustrated with the inability of his class to provide a satisfactory answer. In the end he dragged a student over to the window and pointed to the sky before pronouncing, in lofty tones: 'Mozart is *sunshine!*' As his most celebrated pupil and future son-in-law Josef Suk remarked: 'Sometimes I could howl, but we learn a lot from it.' There was, not surprisingly, a high drop-out rate from his classes, but many of those who stayed the course, including Suk himself and the leading Czech composers Vítězslav Novák and Oskar Nedbal, looked back on Dvořák's tuition as the making of them.

Dvořák in his doctoral gown, Cambridge, 1891

In June 1891 Dvořák and his wife travelled to England once again, for the degree ceremony at Cambridge. The day before the conferral of the honorary doctorate in music the composer conducted his *Stabat mater* and his Sixth Symphony at an afternoon concert in Cambridge, and on 16 June he received the degree itself. Dvořák was overawed by the traditional trappings of the ceremony, for which the university authorities seem to have been lax in preparing him. In particular, the fact that the proceedings were conducted entirely in Latin, a language he had never learnt, meant that he had very little idea what was going on or what he was supposed to do (though later he consoled himself with the thought that 'to compose *Stabat mater* was, after all, better than to know Latin'). The Dvořáks stayed with Stanford, who – evidently not an early riser – recorded in his diary how he was woken 'in the small hours' by a noise in the garden and looked out to find Antonín and Anna sitting under a tree at six o'clock in the morning.

1891 was the year of Dvořák's fiftieth birthday, an anniversary marked by a series of special concerts of his works in Prague, including gala performances of *The Jacobin* and *Dimitrij*. His actual birthday, 8 September, was an occasion of national celebration, from which, however, Dvořák characteristically absented himself in order to spend the day at home with his family in Vysoká.

A month later he returned to England to conduct the first performance of his *Requiem* for four soloists, choir and orchestra, Op. 89 (B.165), at the Birmingham Festival. On his first visit to England seven years earlier Dvořák had hoped that, where he and his music were concerned, the English concert-going public would live up to their reputation for faithfulness to those they had taken a liking to. Certainly the warm reception accorded to the *Requiem* in Birmingham suggested that the reputation was well founded. Although the work is by no means deficient in drama, it never aims at theatricality, and perhaps for that reason has not become as regular a feature of concert programmes as the nineteenth-century Requiems of Berlioz, Verdi and Fauré. What it may lack in gesture, however, it more than makes up for in inwardness. The music has remarkable unity, being bound together by what is for Dvořák an unusually omnipresent four-note motto theme, first heard in the opening bars and deriving from his setting of the words 'When will the wave of life carry me away from this world?' ('Kdy vlna života mne ze světa odnese?') in the sixth of the *Love Songs* of 1888. The orchestra is handled with a skill that puts the instrumental writing of the *Stabat mater* in the shade, among the most memorable touches being the broodingly sinister use of the bass clarinet in the 'Hostias'. The *Requiem* is also more conspicuously Slavonic than the *Stabat mater*: the 'Recordare' is a very Bohemian solo quartet, and the unaccompanied vocal passages in the 'Graduale' and the 'Agnus Dei' seem almost to anticipate the textures of Rachmaninov's *Vespers*. More than any of Dvořák's other sacred works, the *Requiem* stands as enduring testimony both to his craftsmanship as a composer and to the depth of his religious convictions.

Dvořák's two visits to England in 1891 would be his last for half a decade. A few days before he left for Cambridge in June he had received a telegram from New York which was to result in a radical redirection of his professional life. Jeannette M. Thurber, the signatory of the telegram, was a formidable force in American cultural life. Trained at the Paris Conservatoire, she was the wife of a grocery millionaire and deployed the family's surplus fortune in various philanthropic ventures, including an American Opera Company which had been intended to provide an English-language alternative to the Metropolitan's US monopoly but had failed after two financially draining years. A more enduring venture was the National Conservatory of Music in America, a body dedicated to the ideal of creating a national American music through the education of talented students, irrespective of race, gender or means – an astonishingly forward-looking approach in 1890s America. The Conservatory was now in its seventh year and, with an eye to the four-hundredth anniversary of Columbus's landing in the Americas in 1892, Mrs Thurber was keen to make a high-profile European appointment as Director. It was this role she offered to Dvořák, together with an annual salary of $15,000 for eight months' work (to include the conducting of ten concerts) and four months' holiday. Thurber was an organiser of exceptional persuasiveness, and where Dvořák was concerned she was no more inclined to take no for an answer than the board of the Prague Conservatoire had been.

It was clear to Dvořák from the first that there were compelling reasons not to give that answer anyway. For one thing, the prestige of such an appointment was considerable, both for the composer himself and for his beloved country. For another, $15,000 was, at contemporary exchange rates, no less than twenty-five times his annual salary at the Prague Conservatoire. There were, however, equally strong reasons for hesitation. It was, after all, only six months since Dvořák had taken up his Prague professorship. Furthermore, he was an increasingly neurotic traveller, having even considered cancelling his appearance in Cambridge on rumours of a flu epidemic in England. Above all, for a man so committed to his family that he was prepared to cold-shoulder his official fiftieth birthday celebrations to be with them, the thought of placing the Atlantic between himself and his children was hard to countenance. On the one hand, the New World was a golden opportunity; on the other, it meant the temporary loss of everything that was dearest and most familiar to him.

It took Dvořák six months to resolve the conflict. Throughout the remainder of the year he pondered the pros and cons with his family, took advice from friends and colleagues, consulted with the directorate of the Prague Conservatoire, and in hard-headed negotiations with Alfred Littleton (whom Mrs Thurber had commissioned to act as intermediary) ran through draft after draft of a two-year contractual agreement. In December, in a disarmingly frank letter to Thurber written in English, he wrote that while he felt sure of himself as a teacher and conductor there were 'many other trifles which will make me much sorrow and grieve – but I rely on your kindness and indulgence and be sure I shall do all to please you'. Finally, just before Christmas 1891, he signed on the dotted line, and the scene was set for the most unlikely transformation of his career. From September 1892 the taciturn butcher's son from the backwaters of central Europe would be standard-bearer for the musical ambitions of a nation fast establishing itself as the very embodiment of the modern age.

Chapter 6

In the New World
(1892–1895)

...they stopped at Niagara where,
after staring at the falls in silence
for five minutes, he remarked,
'By God! That will be a symphony
in B minor!'

In the New World (1892–1895)

The United States in 1892 was still *terra incognita* for the vast majority of European musicians. It was also a country in search of its own musical voice. Some leading European figures, such as Anton Seidl in New York and Arthur Nikisch in Boston, had recently moved to America and were building successful careers there, but the traffic was mostly the other way, as young musicians left to serve their apprenticeship in the Old World. New York could boast world-class institutions such as the Metropolitan Opera and the New York Philharmonic Orchestra, but they were still heavily dependent on Europe for their leadership and repertoire. Like so many areas of the nation's life in the 1890s, American music was in the throes of an identity crisis. It was Jeannette Thurber's dream that future generations of American musicians could be trained at home, and that by drinking at the fountainhead of their country's musical traditions they could create a genuinely American form of art-music. But she had to turn to the Old World to realise her vision of artistic self-sufficiency for the New.

Dvořák's accession to the directorship of the National Conservatory was therefore not only a new beginning for the composer himself, it also symbolised, in intention if not ultimately in effect, the beginning of a new epoch in American musical life. No composer of his standing had ever been appointed by an American academy before. At Dvořák's first concert on American soil, which took place as part of the country's quatercentennial celebrations, the groundbreaking nature of his arrival was summed up in the title of the welcoming speech given by the millionaire patron Colonel Henry Lee Higginson: 'Two New Worlds – the New World of Columbus and the New World of Music.' Dvořák was there, said Higginson, to graft the latter onto the former. Much of this seems to have come as a surprise to the composer himself. Indeed, he might have hesitated even longer before sending the contract off in December 1891 had he known quite how inflated were the hopes being entertained of him on the other side of the Atlantic.

In the nine months between signing the agreement and his departure for the United States, Dvořák did far more than put his home affairs in order. First of all, in January 1892, he completed the last of a triptych of concert overtures he had been working on for much of the preceding year. He had originally conceived these works as a 'triple overture' under the umbrella title *Nature, Life and Love* ('Příroda, Život a Láska'). His intentions evolved with the music, however, and in the event he gave the overtures the individual titles *In Nature's Realm* ('V přírodě'), *Carnival* ('Karneval') and *Othello*, Opp. 91, 92 and 93 (B.168, 169 & 174). Like his late symphonic poems, the works are programmatic in character, even if here the programmes are as fluid as his titling. Only in the last of the overtures, *Othello*, did he provide pointers to an underlying story, with side-headings in the score such as 'They embrace blissfully', 'Jealousy and a thirst for revenge mature in Othello' and 'Othello murders her in frenzied rage'. Even here, though, his (very free) adaptation of the Shakespearian original is guided as much by musical as by narrative considerations – so much so, in fact, that at one stage he considered renaming the overture 'Eroica'. All three overtures are linked by the 'Nature' theme which first appears in the pastoral opening bars of *In Nature's Realm* (and which has a similar contour to the 'Morning' theme of Grieg's *Peer Gynt*), but they are rarely performed as a single concert item, the ebullient *Carnival* being far the most often heard.

Even before *Othello* was finished, Dvořák had begun a farewell tour of Bohemia, which took him to some forty towns in five months. The centrepiece of most of these appearances was the *Dumky* trio, in which he played the piano with Ferdinand Lachner on the violin and Hanuš Wihan on the cello. (Publicity photos show them to have made a rather dapper trio.) He also rustled up several smaller pieces for cello and piano for the tour, including the Rondo in G minor, Op. 94 (B.171), and arrangements of the last Slavonic dance of the Op. 46 set and 'Silent Woods' ('Klid') from his 1884 piano pieces *From the Bohemian Forest*; like *Klid*, the Rondo was later also arranged for cello and orchestra. There were valedictory concerts to conduct too, in Olomouc, Kroměříž and Prague, and his teaching engagements to complete at the Prague Conservatoire.

Dvořák spent the summer months at Vysoká with his soon to be fragmented family. Anna would be accompanying him to the United States, as would Otilie and Antonín, now fourteen and nine respectively, but the couple's other four children, ranging in age from four to twelve, were to remain behind in Bohemia with their maternal grandmother. It was not just his personal sadness at the prospect of separation that lent Vysoká an unwontedly sombre air that summer. The area was in mourning following a disaster in the nearby silver mines at Příbram, some of the victims of which had been Dvořák's drinking companions at the local inn. There is no hint of tragedy, however, in the music he was writing at the time – his *Te Deum*, Op. 103 (B.176) – for two soloists, choir and orchestra. On the contrary, it is one of his most glad-hearted works. The opening is a spontaneous blaze of jubilation, which returns after a cloudless Sanctus for soprano, chorus and orchestra. The interpolations of the choir into the bass solo 'Tu Rex gloriae' which follows are especially beatific. The ensuing choral 'Aeterna fac cum sanctis tuis' functions as a sort of quasi-symphonic scherzo, and the work ends with another outburst of joy in the glory of God. The most Bohemian in spirit of Dvořák's sacred works, the *Te Deum* was written for his American debut concert at Carnegie Hall in October: Jeannette Thurber had wanted him to present a setting of Joseph Rodman Drake's patriotic poem *The American Flag* at this event, but the text was held up on its way to him, and by the time Dvořák finished the setting in the New Year the Carnegie Hall audience had already heard the more characteristic work.

Dvořák, Anna and the two children left Prague on 15 September 1892. Also travelling with them was a twenty-two-year-old violinist, Josef Jan Kovařík, who was returning home to the United States after completing his studies at the Prague Conservatoire and to whom posterity is indebted for his published recollections of life as a lodger-cum-general-factotum to the Dvořák family in America. The party sailed from Bremen two days later on the SS *Saale*. Seasoned by his shuttlings across the English Channel, the composer was the only passenger to weather the three-day storm that hit them in mid-Atlantic, striding up and down on deck and smoking cigars at the captain's table while the others huddled below in their cabins.

After a day's quarantine on Staten Island, the *Saale* arrived at Hoboken, New Jersey on 27 September, and Dvořák was welcomed at the dockside by Edmund Stanton, the Secretary of the National Conservatory, and a delegation of Czech

327 East 17th Street (on the right), where Dvořák and his family lived in New York

well-wishers. Stanton whisked the travellers into the city by carriage and introduced them to their suite at the Clarendon Hotel on Union Square, where a grand piano had been installed in readiness.

New York in 1892 was not yet the architectural symbol of modernity that it would become in the following century, but it was a metropolis on the grand scale, and Dvořák was duly impressed. Letters home record the throng of shipping in the harbour – soon to become an obsession to rival his interest in trains – the size, beauty and cleanliness of the streets, and the fact that the head of the Statue of Liberty could accommodate a banquet of sixty people. He was less impressed by the noise from the street outside the hotel, and least of all by the cost of living: the expense of the Clarendon rooms was an early indicator that, whatever the dollar–gulden exchange rate, the purchasing power of his new salary fell some way short of its conversion value. Within weeks the Dvořáks and Kovařík moved out of the hotel and into a rented house at 327 East 17th Street, facing Stuyvesant Park, which would be their New York home for the remainder of the composer's time in America.

If Dvořák had failed to realise the extent to which he would be the public face of Thurber's ambitions for American music, the ardent press coverage of his arrival provided brisk enlightenment. 'What the American papers write about me is simply terrible – ' he wrote home, 'they see in me, they say, the saviour of music and I don't know what else besides!' It was a role for which he was less qualified by temperament than by his image as a 'nationalist' composer, but he embraced it with genuine conviction, writing or putting his name to articles on the future of American music, familiarising himself with Native American folk music and listening to Negro spirituals sung for him by the African-American Conservatory student Henry Thacker Burleigh. He was a conscientious, if still eccentric, teacher of his handpicked pupils, some of whom came from as far afield as San Francisco, and he made no complaint at adding the adjudication of nationwide composition competitions to his contractual workload. As a child of the central European lower orders, he was also impressed by what he saw as the relative classlessness of American society: the less well-off were admitted to public rehearsals of some of his concerts, and the Conservatory itself was founded on democratic principles that would have seemed progressive even in the early 1960s. In short, he rose to the challenge of his new role with an energetic sense of vocation. 'The Americans expect great things of me,' he wrote to the Hlávkas in Prague:

I am to show them the way into the Promised Land, the realm of a new, independent art, in short a national style of music!... This will certainly be a great and lofty task, and I hope that with God's help I shall succeed in it.

What the expectations vested in him meant for his profile in the United States was graphically illustrated on 9 October when Dvořák arrived at the Central Turn Verein Opera House for a concert and banquet to welcome him to New York. On his entrance 3,600 Czechs gave him a standing ovation, and he had to make a speech of thanks from the platform, clutching a tributary silver wreath. Twelve days later, scenes of similar enthusiasm greeted his appearance at Carnegie Hall – a new venue with impeccable Slavic associations: Tchaikovsky had been a guest conductor at its opening concert the previous year. Following the obligatory rendition of *My Country, 'Tis of Thee* (after more than a century of independence still sung to the tune of *God Save the Queen*) and, less predictably, Liszt's *Tasso*, Dvořák conducted his three overtures *In Nature's Realm*, *Carnival* and *Othello* and the first performance of the *Te Deum*. It was after this concert that Higginson gave his 'Two New Worlds' speech of welcome to the composer. The American press prided itself on its independence of mind and, as tended to be the case throughout Dvořák's time in the United States, the tone of the reviews – notably those of the polymathic critic of the *New York Tribune*, Henry E. Krehbiel – was thoughtful and analytical rather than exuberant. But there was no mistaking the depth of the goodwill towards him and the project he represented.

In November Dvořák travelled to Boston to conduct his *Requiem*, first at a public rehearsal and then, the following day, at a concert of what he called 'the wealthy and the intelligentsia'. It was rapturously received. He also conducted the Sixth Symphony at a Philharmonic Society concert in New York on 17 December. For the most part, though, his life settled into a routine determined by his duties at the Conservatory, where he held composition classes three days a week and conducted the Conservatory orchestra twice a week. Like thousands of Czech immigrants before him, he created around himself a sort of surrogate Bohemia, transplanting his home regimen as nearly as possible to the overwhelming environment of New York. He got up early, walked in Central Park, inspected the pigeons in the aviary there, and drank coffee with friends at the Manhattan equivalent of his regular

Prague café. More difficult to recreate were his regular visits to the Prague railway stations: in New York no one was allowed onto the platforms at Grand Central station unless they were actually travelling. At first Kovařík would accompany Dvořák for an hour's journey on the overhead railway to 155th Street where, in one of the more bizarre images from the annals of late Romanticism, the fiery-eyed, wild-bearded composer and his young assistant would spend the whole afternoon sitting on an embankment watching the trains go by. Later Dvořák found a substitute for his locomotive interests in the transatlantic steamships that plied their trade from New York harbour. On sailing days the public was allowed on board, and Dvořák had soon explored every ship and made friends with captains and crew alike. When the ships sailed, he would watch them until they were out of sight, sometimes taking the overhead railway to Battery Park for the purpose, and would follow their subsequent progress in the shipping columns of the newspapers. Dvořák's daily routine also entailed his going to bed early, as a result of which he accepted few of the invitations that came his way and was an infrequent concertgoer. He barely visited the Met, and when Seidl gave him tickets for a performance of *Siegfried* there, he and Kovařík turned up embarrassingly early and in informal suits only to find themselves in the Diamond Horseshoe; here, as became clear when the rest of the audience began to arrive, evening dress was the order of the day. They skulked at the back of their box and left at the first interval. New York seems also to have exacerbated Dvořák's agoraphobia, further curtailing his social life. Mrs Thurber must sometimes have wondered what she had taken on.

But Dvořák was also composing. Two days after completing *The American Flag* (B.177) in January 1893 he began work on his first all-American composition, the Symphony No. 9 in

CD 2 5

143

E minor, Op. 95 (B.178), which occupied him until 24 May. Later in the year, just before he sent off the score to Seidl, who was to give the premiere, Dvořák scribbled on the front page the words 'Z nového světa', giving the symphony the flag under which it has sailed ever since: 'From the New World'.

More than any other single composition, it is to the 'New World' Symphony that Dvořák owes his popular fame. The work is one of that élite company of nineteenth-century symphonies never to have been out of the repertoire since its first performance and is one of the best-known pieces in the entire canon of classical music. It is also one of Dvořák's most debated works. In particular, his off-the-cuff title has focused attention even more than the circumstances of its composition on the extent to which it draws on American folk sources. Dvořák himself claimed that the words meant simply 'impressions and greetings from the New World' and that the

Sketch of the scherzo from the 'New World' Symphony

symphony was as thoroughly Bohemian as any of his mature works. ('It seems that I have got them all confused,' Kovařík reported him saying. 'At home they will understand at once what I meant.') At the same time it shares with other works of his American period – such as 'The American' Quartet and the String Quintet in E flat major – a distinctive musical flavour which is at least in part derived from the traditional African-American and Native American (in nineteenth-century terms Negro and Red Indian) music with which he had been making himself familiar since his arrival in the United States. Indeed, just three days before he finished the symphony the *New York Herald* published an interview with the composer in which he was reported as saying:

I am now satisfied that the future music of this country must be founded upon what are called the negro melodies... In the negro melodies of America I discover all that is needed for a great and noble school of music. They are pathetic, tender, passionate, melancholy, solemn, religious, bold, merry, gay or what you will. It is music that suits itself to any mood or any purpose. There is nothing in the whole range of composition that cannot be supplied with themes from this source.

Similarities can certainly be found between some of Dvořák's thematic material and African-American spirituals: the G major flute theme in the first movement, for example, is famously reminiscent of 'Swing low, sweet chariot', and the cor anglais melody of the *Largo* is so like a spiritual that it was actually turned into one, under the title 'Goin' home'. But there is little evidence to suggest that Dvořák was consciously drawing on specific spirituals or Native American themes in composing the symphony, any more than he drew on specific Czech folk melodies for the *Slavonic Dances*. Rather, as he said in another article in the *New York Herald*, published to coincide with the first performance of the symphony in December 1893, through studying 'the music of the Negroes and the Indians' he had become 'imbued with their characteristics – with their spirit, in fact'.

> *It is this spirit which I have tried to reproduce in my Symphony. I have not actually used any of the melodies. I have simply written original themes embodying the peculiarities of the Indian music, and, using these themes as subjects, have developed them with all the resources of modern rhythms, harmony, counterpoint and orchestral color.*

The first movement, he said, 'embodies the principles which I have already worked out in my Slavonic Dances; that is, to preserve, to translate into music, the spirit of a race as distinct in its national melodies or folk songs'.

As samples of Dvořák's English-language correspondence will have shown, such accounts are far from being editorially unmediated; nor did the lexicon of ethnomusicology come naturally to him. But for all the fierce debate that has swirled around such pronouncements, both at the time and since, the December interview rings absolutely true to the listening experience of the 'New World' Symphony. The 'peculiarities' can be analysed, as Dvořák and many later critics analysed them, in terms of pentatonic scales, flattened leading notes and syncopated rhythms. In the end, however, what conveys itself to the hearer is an unmistakable but intangible 'spirit' of Americanism, which distinguishes the symphony and other works of Dvořák's time in the United States from those on either side of them.

The formal structure of the Ninth Symphony has also been the subject of much critical comment. As in the *Requiem*, all

the movements are linked by variants of a motto theme, which makes its first appearance as the principal subject of the first movement; but here the device is handled with less subtlety, and the reappearance of all the main themes of the work in the finale has an uncomfortably mechanistic feel. There is, as Julius Harrison has remarked, a 'patchwork' quality to the symphony, reflecting both its musical procedures and, perhaps, the disparate sources of its inspiration. Dvořák described the slow movement, for example, as 'a study or sketch for a longer work' based on Longfellow's dramatic poem *The Song of Hiawatha*, which Jeannette Thurber had been urging on him as an opera subject (she had even taken

The Dvořák family, shortly after arriving in America, 1892

147

him to see the Indians dance at Buffalo Bill's Wild West show) and which remains the great might-have-been of his time in America. Similarly, he associated the scherzo with the dance of Pau-Puk-Keewis at the wedding feast in Chapter 11 of Longfellow's poem. But if the 'New World' is not the most finely wrought of Dvořák's symphonies, it has a freshness and immediacy that went straight to the hearts of its first-night audience, and have enchanted music lovers ever since.

With the completion of his symphony, Dvořák also came to the end of his first academic year at the National Conservatory. Under the terms of his agreement with Mrs Thurber he was due four months' paid holiday, and it had originally been his intention to take this back home in Vysoká. He had, however, become fascinated by Kovařík's accounts of

Spillville, Iowa, his home village, the little Czech community of Spillville in *where Dvořák and* north-east Iowa, and had decided to spend the summer there *his family spent the* instead. He therefore arranged for the rest of his family to join *summer of 1893* him, and on the very day that he finished the symphony he

heard that Anna, Magda, Otakar and Zinda had arrived safely in England on the first leg of their journey to the New World. The story that this exciting news made him forget to complete the trombone parts of the symphony is sadly apocryphal, but the last page of the autograph score bears the inscription: 'Praise God! Completed 24th May 1893 at 9 o'clock in the morning. The children have arrived at Southampton (a cable came at 1.33 pm).' A week later, accompanied by their aunt Terezie Koutecká and a nanny, they disembarked in New York, and on 3 June the whole Dvořák caravan set off on the 1,300-mile journey to Iowa.

Freed from his responsibilities at the Conservatory and the oppressive bustle of New York, and with his whole family around him for the first time in eight months, Dvořák gradually began to unwind. Travelling via Philadelphia, Harrisburgh and the Allegheny Mountains to Pittsburgh and Chicago, he became more and more interested in the country they were passing through, bombarding the ever-patient Kovařík with questions about everything he saw from the window of the train. At Chicago they were welcomed by Kovařík's brother, who showed them round the city. Then in the evening they continued their journey, arriving the next morning at McGregor, Iowa, where they had their first sight of the Mississippi. The train deposited them at Calmar, the nearest station to Spillville, where they were met by a carriage and joined for the last few miles of the journey by two parish priests and Kovařík's father, who in true Bohemian fashion was the Spillville schoolmaster and choirmaster.

Spillville was a prairie settlement of some 350 souls, most of them first- or second-generation Czech immigrants. Despite its isolation and the unfamiliar landscape of the Mid-West, Dvořák felt instantly at home here. The rhythms of daily life were those of Nelahozeves and Vysoká – farmwork, Mass, visits to neighbours – and he was surrounded by Czech voices and Czech names. Whereas in New York his countryman's routine seemed even more out of place than in Prague, in Spillville it made natural sense again. He rose at four in the morning and walked for an hour before sitting down to work. At seven he attended church, then worked and walked again before spending much of the afternoon chatting to the older settlers about their early experiences of life in the American Mid-West, where many of them had combined agricultural work with labouring jobs on the railway. For the first time since his arrival in the United States he heard rural birdsong, and he revelled in the unfamiliar calls. He even broke with his normal practice to note one down – probably that of the scarlet tanager – and used it in his next composition, the String Quartet No. 12 in F major. On his very first day in Spillville he surprised the congregation of the little church, St Wenceslas, by sitting down at the organ to play the Czech hymn *Bože, před tvou velebností* ('God, before Thy majesty'), and throughout the remainder of his stay he continued to play the organ or lead the choir at Mass. This was Vysoká-in-Iowa, and he was genuinely at ease for the first time in America. Kovařík noted that Dvořák even lost the nervous phobias that afflicted him in the city: he no longer needed to be accompanied on his walks, and the good folk of Spillville often had no idea where he had gone.

The Dvořáks lodged in an unprepossessing block of a house found for them by the parish priest, Father Tomáš Bílý, who became a great friend. It was here, almost as soon as the family had unpacked, that Dvořák began what remains far and away the best known of his chamber works, the String Quartet No. 12 in F major, Op. 96 (B.179) 'The American'. Dvořák always told Simrock that he could compose only when he was in the right mood, and however disingenuous the claim, there can be no surer indication of his happiness at Spillville than the fact that he completed the sketches of the quartet in just three days and the whole work less than a fortnight later. 'Thanks to the Lord God. I am satisfied,' he wrote at the end of the sketch. 'It went quickly.'

'The American' Quartet has the same immediacy of appeal as the 'New World' Symphony. Indeed the two works, together with his next Spillville work, the String Quintet in E flat major, and the Sonatina for violin and piano that he wrote on his return to New York, seem closer to one another in their musical DNA than they are to their nearest relatives in the rest of Dvořák's output. Here too there are African-American and Native American inflections, and once again the sense of difference is more easily felt than defined. The whole work could aptly bear the epigraph of the first movement of Beethoven's 'Pastoral' Symphony, 'Awakening of happy feelings on arrival in the country'. The framing movements are infectiously joyful, the scarlet tanager pops up in a stratospherically high violin motif in the scherzo, and the slow movement conveys a sense of breadth at once expansive and slightly oppressive, in which it is surely not fanciful to sense the vast distances of the Mid-Western prairie under the intense summer heat. It seems wholly appropriate that the quartet – like Spillville itself, a happy confluence of the Czech and the American – should have had its first hearing not in an urban concert hall but in a run-through at the hands of the Kovaříks and the composer himself in a house in the village where it was written.

While Dvořák was at work on the quartet a group of Native Americans, under the leadership of the magnificently monikered Big Moon, passed through Spillville on a trading expedition. This was the so-called Kickapoo medicine show, a well-rehearsed commercial enterprise and as such hardly the purest fount of traditional song and dance; but the unfamiliar music was fascinating to Dvořák. At one of the party's performances at the village inn Kovařík noted down a figure that seems to have been the inspiration for a theme (the second subject of the first movement) in Dvořák's next American work, the String Quintet in E flat major, Op. 97 (B.180), which he began just three days after finishing 'The American' Quartet. The quintet too has been known as 'The American', and the fast movements share several of the distinctive features of the quartet and the 'New World' Symphony, including the radical simplification of musical language which characterises Dvořák's interest in American folk sources: the atmosphere of the trio in the second movement, for example, is markedly similar to that of the quartet's slow movement. These features are least evident in the *Larghetto*, which in its classicism seems almost to belong to a different work: it is a set of five variations on the earliest theme to appear in Dvořák's American notebooks, the hymn-like second half of which he apparently conceived as the basis for a new setting of *My Country, 'Tis of Thee*.

The day after Dvořák began the quintet, there occurred back in New York an event that would prove of pivotal significance both in the history of the United States and in the composer's own American career. For all its apparent prosperity, America in the 1890s was a deeply divided society. Behind the ethnomusicological debates over Negro spirituals and Red Indian music, beneath the rural idyll of Spillville and the liberal philanthropy of the Thurbers, lay the turbulent realities of an age of rapid and barely regulated industrialisation. The visionary egalitarianism of the National Conservatory stood in stark contrast to the all-out assault on the civil rights of African-Americans in the Southern states, which left millions effectively disenfranchised by the end of the decade. Likewise, the Native American songs that Dvořák enjoyed in the inn at Spillville were the bastardised remnants of a culture whose last hopes of independence had been bloodily crushed at Wounded Knee just two-and-a-half years earlier. Again, Dvořák's conversations with his Spillville neighbours must have touched on the formation the previous year of the Populist Party, the political voice of an agrarian crisis which had already seen thousands of farmers abandon their land under the combined pressures of drought and falling commodity prices; and while his letters home enthused about democratic relations between the wealthy and their servants, the gap between rich and poor was growing ever wider as the 'robber barons' of American commerce built up their giant monopolies. It was against this background that on 27 June 1893 the New York stock market crashed, wiping millions of dollars off share values and triggering widespread financial panic. By the end of the year hundreds of banks had closed their doors and thousands of businesses had collapsed. The shockwaves from these seismic events were to unsettle, and finally undermine, the foundations of Dvořák's presence in America; for among the East Coast millionaires suddenly exposed to the cold winds of economic depression were the Thurbers themselves.

Meanwhile, at the beginning of August, the Dvořák family paid a week-long visit to one of the great tourist attractions of the age, the World Columbian Exposition in Chicago. The fair was mounted on a gargantuan scale – 'truly "made in America",' Dvořák observed – and included such architectural set pieces as a huge artificial lake surrounded by neo-classical buildings. Dvořák wrote to his old friend Antonín Rus about the pageantry of 'Bohemian Day', 12 August, when 30,000 American Czechs processed from the city to the Exposition, and a concert was given at which he conducted his Eighth

Symphony to ecstatic applause from an audience of 8,000. (A portrait of him conducting at this event captures the woodenness of his rostrum stance so often commented on by admirers and detractors alike.) Ominously, however, even this grand enterprise was not immune from the economic turmoil of the times: Dvořák reported to Rus that the Exposition as a whole was losing money.

At the beginning of September he, Anna and Kovařík went on a thousand-mile sightseeing tour to Omaha, Nebraska, where they visited the Bohemian-born newspaper magnate Edward Rosewater and were lavishly entertained by the local Czech community, then on to St Paul, Minnesota, which was also home to a large population of Czech immigrants. From St Paul they visited the spectacular Minnehaha Falls, where Dvořák noted down on his shirt cuff a theme soon to be used in the slow movement of his next American composition, the Sonatina for violin and piano. Waterfalls seem particularly to have inspired him. On the family's return journey to New York a couple of weeks later they stopped at Niagara where, after staring at the falls in silence for five minutes, he remarked, 'By God! That will be a symphony in B minor!' – an observation that might be more plausible as the genesis of the Cello Concerto in B minor had the first sketches of that great work not been made in D minor. In the event, all that survived of the idea is a theme in the last of the eight *Humoresques* for piano which Dvořák composed a year later.

After the peace and contentment of Spillville, Dvořák's return to his duties in New York at the beginning of his second academic year at the Conservatory seems to have reactivated all his urban anxieties. It would no doubt have been an even more stressful experience but for the fact that the whole family stayed on in America with him. The children were enrolled in local schools, and Dvořák's delight at having them around him again found intimate expression in his first composition of the new term, the Sonatina in G major for violin and piano (B.183), which he dedicated to all his children and gave the talismanic (if strictly inaccurate) opus number 100. The Sonatina belongs recognisably to the sound world of the Ninth Symphony, 'The American' Quartet and 'The American' Quintet. The pentatonic first subject of the opening movement even becomes reminiscent of the song 'Clementine' in the development section. The *Larghetto*, which, with its languorous theme from the Minnehaha Falls, has often been detached from the work and played under the fanciful title 'Indian Lament', has a section redolent of the strumming of campfire guitars. There are suggestions of the hoedown in the scherzo's energetic fiddling, and a wonderfully reposeful episode amid the barn dance drive of the finale.

On 9 December 1893 Otilie wrote to her godfather Göbl about the fun she and Toník were having playing their new sonatina in the East 17th Street house. Exactly a week later Dvořák was present when Anton Seidl conducted the premiere of the 'New World' Symphony at a memorable Philharmonic Society concert in Carnegie Hall. (The work had in fact been heard at a public rehearsal the previous evening, but this was the official first performance.) In a career of triumphs this concert represents a high-water mark of public appreciation for Dvořák and his music. The *New York Herald* captured the electric atmosphere in an article the following day, describing the spontaneous eruption of applause after the second movement and how when Seidl gestured towards the composer's box the entire audience craned their necks to catch sight of the hero of the hour:

At last a broad shouldered individual of medium height,
and as straight as one of the pines in the forests of which

*his music whispered so eloquently, is descried by the eager
watchers. A murmur sweeps through the hall. 'Dvořák!
Dvořák' is the word that passes from mouth to mouth...
With hands trembling with emotion Dr. Dvořák waves
an acknowledgment of his indebtedness to Anton Seidl,
to the orchestra, to the audience, and then disappears into
the background while the remainder of the work goes on...
At its close the composer was loudly called for. Again and
again he bowed his acknowledgments, and again and again
the applause burst forth. Even after he had left his box and
was walking about in the corridor the applause continued.
And finally he returned to the gallery railing, and then what
a reception he received! The musicians, led by Mr. Seidl,
applauded until the place rang again.*

Dvořák wrote with laconic good humour to Simrock, with
whom he had resumed cordial relations during the summer:

*the newspapers write that no composer has ever had such
success... the people applauded so much that I had to thank
them from the box like a king (!?) à la Mascagni in Vienna
(don't laugh!). You know that I like to keep clear of such
ovations but I had to do it and to show myself!*

As this letter suggests, the calculated waiting game Dvořák
had played since his severance of relations with Simrock three
years earlier had had the desired result. As he wrote to Rus
from Spillville: 'At last Simrock has eaten humble pie, and says
he will take all my works. I was sure he would have to come
to me first and not I to him.' The works in question included
the 'New World' Symphony, 'The American' Quartet, the
Dumky trio and the three overtures, and Simrock not only
bought them sight unseen but also published their titles in

both Czech and German. It was a minor triumph for Dvořák to set alongside the staggering success of his new symphony in the United States and, soon, throughout the world.

Not long after the 'New World' premiere, Dvořák gave an interview to the *New York Herald* in which he laid out the principles behind his teaching. The article, published in January 1894 under the headline 'How Dr. Dvorak gives a lesson', provides an important insight into his own creative practice, and a healthy corrective to the stylised image of Dvořák as a kind of musical innocent, somehow drawing his music directly from the sights and sounds of nature. This is the voice of a highly conscious, rationally self-critical artist. For the reticent Dvořák it is also a rare example of an extended creative credo, and is worth quoting at length:

> *Have a reason for everything you do. Examine your reason from every point of view. Make up your mind as to the merit of a musical theme, its treatment or its accompaniment, only after careful thorough consideration. Then, having come to a decided opinion on the matter, set to work and write it out. You may find many things to change upon further reflection, you may modify the work in many ways, but if your reasoning has been thorough you will find that the foundation, the kernel, of your work remains just the same. I have no patience with the people who write down the first thing that comes into their head, who accompany it with the harmonies that happen to suggest themselves at the moment, who then score it for any instrument, or combination of instruments, that catches their fancy without any regard to effect! There would not be so much nonsense written if people thought more...*
>
> *You must not imitate. Model your style upon all that is best, all that is noble and elevated in the literature of music,*

*but remain yourself. Do not become the copyist of anyone,
for you will invariably copy your model's defects, while his
merits will be so subtle that they will escape you.*

How many people, knowing only the music, would recognise
its composer in these words? Yet time and again Dvořák's
notebooks and sketches bear witness to their truth, with
even the most natural-sounding themes often emerging
only after laborious shaping and reshaping. Indeed, there
can be few more telling examples of art hiding art than the
apparently spontaneous flow of sound we think of as Dvořák's
characteristic gift.

Another illuminating excursion into journalism also
belongs to 1894. The article on Schubert that Dvořák co-
wrote for *The Century Illustrated Monthly Magazine* is his
longest analysis of another composer's music, but it is hard
not to read it also as an essay on the limits of self-knowledge.
Indeed, its criticisms of Schubert, whom Dvořák loved, are
so uncannily similar to those most frequently levelled at his
own music that one almost suspects his co-author, Henry T.
Finck, of a mischievous editorial hand. Of the symphonies,
for example, Dvořák/Finck opines that if they have 'a serious
fault it is prolixity; he does not know when to stop', and, most
strikingly, of the operas:

*He was always unlucky with his librettos, which are, without
exception, inadequate... yet the chief cause of his failure lay,
after all, in the nature of his genius, which was lyrical, and not
dramatic, or, at any rate, not theatrical.*

As he authorised these words, did Dvořák, so often
disappointed in his own theatrical ambitions, really not
wonder if the cap might fit?

As his second year at the Conservatory advanced, Dvořák was faced with a decision. Jeannette Thurber was keen for him to commit to a further year or two when his current contract came to an end. There were good reasons to stay. His music continued to be well received: the Kneisel Quartet, who premiered 'The American' Quartet in Boston on 1 January 1894 and 'The American' Quintet eleven days later at Carnegie Hall, gave fifty performances of the quartet in the course of the next twelve months. Dvořák also remained in full sympathy with the aims of the Conservatory. In January he took part in an all- or almost all-black concert of his own and African-American students' music at the Madison Square concert hall to raise money for casualties of the economic depression (the programme included an arrangement he had just made of Stephen Foster's sentimental standard *Old Folks at Home*).

But there were forceful counter-pressures too. He was so homesick that when Terezie Koutecká boarded her ship back to Europe in February he wept at being unable to return with her. There were also ominous signs that the financial crisis of the previous summer was percolating through to the Thurbers' own fortunes. Salary payments began to arrive late or were not honoured at the bank, and by April 1894 the irregularities had become so serious that Dvořák wrote to Mrs Thurber threatening, albeit regretfully, to expose the situation to the press if he was not paid according to contract. The tactic worked in the short term, but it was hardly the most comfortable background against which to be making crucial decisions about his future. Dvořák was further unsettled by the deaths in November 1893 and February 1894 of his friends Tchaikovsky and von Bülow, and by the news that his seventy-nine-year-old father was seriously ill in Velvary, the market town from which the young Toník had herded that recalcitrant heifer so many years before.

It was against this unpromising background that Dvořák composed one of his least occluded confections, the five-movement Suite in A major for piano, Op. 98 (B.184). Often unaccountably regarded as the poor relation in Dvořák's family of American works – in stark contrast to the composer's own valuation – the suite was written between 19 February and 1 March 1894 but is better known in the orchestral version he made the following year (B.190). There is much in its musical language to proclaim its kinship with Dvořák's other American compositions, but Bohemian elements are more to the fore – most especially in the hectic second movement, while in the wistful penultimate *Andante* Dvořák's eyes seem still to be following Terezie's ship as it makes its way over the horizon.

Of greater significance, however, are the ten settings of psalm texts from the Bible of Kralice that Dvořák made for voice and piano immediately after completing the suite. The *Biblical Songs* ('Biblické písně'), Op. 99 (B.185), the first five of which he orchestrated in January 1895, are among the finest of all Dvořák's songs and a profound expression of faith at a time when his mind was much occupied with mortality and the trials of earthly life. There is a special, and surely personal, intensity to the seventh song, in which Dvořák sets the first five verses of Psalm 137, with its ageless cry of the exile: 'By the rivers of Babylon, there we sat down, yea, we wept, when we remembered Zion... How shall we sing the Lord's song in a strange land?' Dvořák finished the songs on 26 March. Two days later František died in Velvary. The distance separating his son from home must have seemed vaster than ever.

Finally, on 19 May 1894, Dvořák and his family boarded the SS *Aller* for Europe at the end of his first stay in America. Four days earlier he had swallowed his doubts and signed a second two-year contract with the National Conservatory,

Dvořák in 1894

on the understanding that his teaching engagements would be limited to six months in the first year. For the moment, though, all he wanted was to see Vysoká again, even if it meant absenting himself from some of the official celebrations mounted to welcome the returning hero to Prague. When he finally arrived in the village on 4 June he was greeted by a torchlight procession of his friends and neighbours. In thanksgiving for his safe return he donated a new organ to the parish church at nearby Třebsko, dedicating it on his fifty-third birthday in September.

Dvořák spent the summer at Vysoká, surrounded by his family, his pigeons and his beloved Bohemian countryside. It would have been an altogether cloudless homecoming but for the fact that his beloved sister-in-law Josefina was suffering from a deteriorating heart condition. Apart from a revision of *Dimitrij* which he had begun in the United States, all Dvořák wrote during these months of relaxation was a set of eight *Humoresques* ('Humoresky') for piano, Op. 101 (B.187), and two other piano pieces (B.188) which were published only in 1911.

CD 2 ⑦

The *Humoresques* began life as another set of Scottish dances to add to those he had composed in 1877, but they quickly outgrew their origins. An elegantly crafted series of miniatures, they deploy several ideas that appear in the American sketchbooks, including in the fourth piece a subject intended to represent Hiawatha as a child. The first piece, which was derived from sketches for a funeral march, would almost fit the Hollywood image of Red Indian music, while the third seems sometimes to stray towards ragtime. The seventh, a *Poco lento e grazioso* in G flat major, has become, serendipitously, one of Dvořák's best-known works and the subject of countless arrangements. The two unassuming piano pieces, B.188 were probably intended to open a second series of *humoresques*. Entitled 'Lullaby' ('Ukolébavka') and 'Capriccio' – the first having a stormy central section that would certainly wake up the baby again! – they are the last works Dvořák composed for the keyboard.

Towards the end of the holiday, after visiting Göbl and Rus, the friends to whom he had written so often from the United States, Dvořák conducted a farewell concert in Prague which included the first performance there of the 'New World' Symphony and, poignantly enough, the overture *My Homeland*. Then on 16 October he left for America, this time accompanied only by Anna and Otakar.

Dvořák might have been forgiven for seeing in the stormy weather against which the SS *Bismarck* battled its way from Southampton to New York an augury for his coming stay. Certainly the auspices were poor for this second visit. Even before he left home he had been involved in some last-minute brinkmanship with Jeannette Thurber when she sent only a quarter rather than the promised half of his outstanding salary. Within weeks of resuming his duties on 1 November he was writing to Rus about the unease the three of them felt at being separated from the rest of the family, and how they waited expectantly for the European ships to dock, bringing their twice-weekly letters from the children back home in Bohemia. Teaching consumed most of his time and energy, leaving uncomfortably little of either for composition. Prompted perhaps by hearing Victor Herbert's Cello Concerto at a concert in New York the previous year, he had begun work on a cello concerto of his own in November, and in the middle of January he complained in a letter home that, whereas at Vysoká he would have finished the whole thing long ago, here in America he was still writing the finale. It was another three weeks before he completed it, on 9 February 1895, noting on the title page that it was Otakar's tenth birthday. He could hardly wait for the end of term. On 16 April, shaving a few days off his contractual six months, the Dvořáks sailed for home. Another augury attended their return voyage: they travelled on the SS *Saale*, the very same ship that had first brought them to the New World two-and-a-half years earlier. Perhaps they already suspected the significance of the symmetry.

CD 2 [8]

The Cello Concerto in B minor, Op. 104 (B.191), is the crowning work of Dvořák's American period and is widely regarded as the greatest concerto ever written for the instrument. The work seems intimately bound up with Dvořák's feelings for his sister-in-law Josefina Kounicová. It may be significant that his only other cello concerto, which remained in short score, was written in 1865, the year he fell in love with her. Certainly when he heard in November 1894 that she was now dangerously ill he included in the second movement of the work the theme of 'Lasst mich allein' ('Leave me alone'), a favourite song of hers from his *Four Songs* Op. 82. Josefina died on 27 May 1895, a month after Dvořák's return to Bohemia. Two days later he attended her funeral, and afterwards rewrote the coda to the concerto's finale to include a further reminiscence of the song as a memorial to her. Despite being composed almost entirely in the United States, the concerto shares little of the musical language of the American works that precede it, as if – intensely as Dvořák felt his separation from friends and family – his creative imagination had already returned to his homeland. Among the Cello Concerto's many admirers was Brahms, who on perusing the score is said to have growled: 'Why on earth didn't I know that one could write a violoncello concerto like this? If I had only known, I would have written one long ago!'

Dvořák was highly protective of the Cello Concerto. Its dedicatee was his old friend and partner on the 1892 *Dumky* trio tour of Bohemia, Hanuš Wihan. However, whereas

Dvořák had gladly accepted the advice of the Violin Concerto's dedicatee, Joseph Joachim, and had made far-reaching changes to the work in consequence, he was incensed by Wihan's attempt to interpolate a cadenza into the last movement of the Cello Concerto. 'The Finale closes gradually *diminuendo*, like a sigh,' he insisted to Simrock, 'with reminiscences of the 1st and 2nd movements – the solo dies down to *pp*, then swells again, and the last bars are taken up by the orchestra and the whole concludes in a stormy mood. That is my idea and I cannot depart from it.'

'I rejoice in God's natural world,' he wrote to Göbl from Vysoká that summer, 'and I am idle and do nothing. You may be surprised at this, but it is the truth, God's truth; I am a lazybones and am not touching my pen.' He had indeed laid aside the first movement of a string quartet in A flat major, begun in his final days in New York. His mind was hardly at rest, however. Reunited with his family, and still owed a quarter of his salary by the National Conservatory (a manifest breach of contract from Jeannette Thurber's side), he was taking advice from Rus, Hlávka and others on the possibility of not returning to the States for the start of the academic year 1895–6. Finally, on 17 August, he wrote Mrs Thurber a letter of resignation, citing family considerations as the basis for his decision. She made no attempt to change his mind. The American chapter of Dvořák's life was closed, and with it a chapter in the history of American music.

Dvořák left behind him in the United States a legacy of continuing influence through the pupils he had taught at the National Conservatory, including Rubin Goldmark (who later became Director of Composition at the Juilliard School, and the teacher of Aaron Copland and George Gershwin) and Harry Rowe Shelley (who went on to teach Charles Ives). The project to create a distinctive national music lost impetus with his departure, however, as did the Conservatory itself. Dvořák's most sympathetic ally in the American press, Henry Krehbiel, was surely telling no more than the sober truth when he wrote, the year after Dvořák's return to Europe, that 'So far as the vast majority of the people of the United States are concerned, it would be entirely proper to say of them that from 1892 to 1895 they entertained an angel in their midst unawares'. But perhaps the last word on Dvořák's New World adventure should go to the woman whose vision it had been. Looking back over decades of association with the Conservatory that she had founded, the indomitable Jeannette Thurber, who lived until after the Second World War, was able to write: 'there is nothing I am so proud of as having been able to bring Dr. Dvorak to America'.

Chapter 7

The Final Flowering (1895–1904)

The G major quartet, in particular, is a work of infinitely rewarding complexity.

The Final Flowering (1895–1904)

When he returned from the United States for the last time Dvořák was not yet fifty-four years old and was at the height of his reputation and creative powers. His music was a staple of concert programmes throughout the world and he was the recipient of honours from civil and musical institutions at home and abroad. His experience of America had expanded if not deepened his musical language, and in the 'New World' Symphony he had created a work already set fair to outstrip everything else he had written in popular acclaim. In the nine years of life left to him he continued to divide his time between Prague and Vysoká, between teaching and composition, and between the demands of public and family life. But the story of these years is, above all, that of the music he wrote during them, and here Dvořák – as always temperamentally incapable of standing still – was about to strike out in a new, and for several of his friends and supporters disconcerting, direction.

The time between his return from America and November 1895, when he resumed his duties at the Prague Conservatoire, was one of his longest periods of creative inactivity. Letters to friends paint a picture of contented indolence among the familiar surroundings of Vysoká, but these months must also have been touched by the restlessness that invariably came over him when he was not composing and, still more, by grief at Josefina's death. There is evidence that, even after he had made the momentous decision not to return to America, this was a time of concentrated reflection for Dvořák as he reacclimatised himself to the patterns of home and musical life in Bohemia after the tensions and excitements of the New World. It would be surprising if the subjects of that reflection had not included the future shape of his music.

In any event, within days of returning to his desk at the Prague Conservatoire Dvořák picked up his pen again. The work in question was not the A flat major String Quartet which he had started and laid aside in the United States, but a new quartet in G major, which occupied him until 9 December. Three days after finishing it he turned back to the hundred or so bars he had written of the A flat quartet, and here too work proceeded with reassuring speed. In a letter to Göbl of 23 December Dvořák reported that he had finished two of the movements and was 'inexpressibly glad' to be spending this Christmas, unlike the previous one, among family and friends; the letter also relates that he had just visited Vienna, where he spent almost all his time with Brahms. The quartet was completed a week later.

The string quartets in G major, Op. 106 (B.192) and A flat major, Op. 105 (B.193) – the opus numbers reflect the order in which they were begun – are Dvořák's last works in the medium and among his finest. Both leave far behind them the quasi primitive idiom of 'The American' Quartet. The G major quartet, in particular, is a work of infinitely rewarding complexity. The opening *Allegro moderato* ranks with Dvořák's greatest achievements in chamber music, while the *Adagio ma non troppo* is one of the most questing movements he ever wrote, both formally and emotionally. Only in the finale does his undiminished appetite for aesthetic exploration lead him into some awkward terrain. The A flat quartet is, if only by comparison, a more modest, relaxed work, its scherzo the happy summation of a lifetime's experience drawing on the folk-dance traditions of the Slavonic lands.

The two quartets are the last pieces of 'absolute music' that Dvořák wrote. From now on his focus would be on 'dramatic composition', a term he applied principally to opera but which equally well describes the programme music to which he turned his mind almost as soon as he completed the A flat quartet. On 6 January 1896 he began work on *The Water Goblin*, the first of four symphonic poems based on ballads by Karel Jaromír Erben, whose collection of folk-tales had already furnished the text for *The Spectre's Bride*. The stories behind the symphonic poems of 1896 are, if anything, even more lurid. *The Water Goblin* ('Vodník'), Op. 107 (B.195) tells the tale of a maiden who is dragged below the surface of a lake by an evil water spirit, by whom she has a child. She persuades the goblin to let her return to her mother, on condition that she leaves the baby in surety of her return by evening. When she lingers beyond the deadline, the goblin emerges from the lake, knocks on the door of her mother's cottage and, after raising a supernatural storm, leaves the baby's decapitated body on the doorstep. In *The Noon Witch* ('Polednice'), Op. 108 (B.196) a mother threatens her mildly troublesome child with the witch of the title, only to have her arrive on cue and kill the child. *The Golden Spinning Wheel* ('Zlatý kolovrat'), Op. 109 (B.197) is the only one of the poems to end happily, but in other respects the story is the most horrific, involving the murder and dismemberment of the heroine by her own stepmother and the separate retrieval of the girl's feet, hands and eyes with the help of the eponymous spinning wheel. In a burst of fertility remarkable even by Dvořák's standards, especially after the fallow months of the previous year, each of these symphonic poems was sketched in a matter of days and all three were completed by 25 April. The fourth, *The Wild Dove* ('Holoubek'), Op. 110 (B.198) was composed between 22 October and 18 November, and is the story of a widow who has poisoned her husband, marries a younger man and is driven to guilty suicide when a dove coos over her first husband's grave.

Quite why Dvořák was drawn to such unremittingly ghoulish fare must remain an open question. In historical hindsight, however, the choice of form, at least, appears less inexplicable than it did to many of his contemporaries. We know that an undiminished admiration for the music of Liszt and Wagner survived Dvořák's youthful experiments in the language and formal precepts of the neo-German school. He is said to have remarked, with characteristic critical intemperance, that 'only what Christ taught and Liszt wrote will endure through the ages'; while his Prague Conservatoire student Josef Michl reports him describing Wagner as 'undefeatable' and comparing him, laterally enough, to Homer. What rekindled his interest now? His friendship with Anton Seidl in America may have played an important part. As a young man in Bayreuth, Seidl had copied the *Ring* score for Wagner and he had remained a passionate Wagnerian ever since. Given the Wagner-drenched atmosphere of 1890s New York musical life, did their Manhattan café conversations perhaps awaken in Dvořák a sense of unfinished business?

There is a clear antecedent for the new, full-bloodedly programmatic direction of the symphonic poems in the three overtures *In Nature's Realm*, *Carnival* and, especially, *Othello*. With the partial exception of the latter, however, there are no precedents in Dvořák's purely instrumental output for the detailed translation of words into music that one finds in the Erben works. In all of them the structure and thematic material are determined to an extraordinary extent by the underlying narratives. The composer told Richter that 'in each one there are three or four characters whom I have made an effort to personalise', and letters provide episode-by-episode breakdowns of *The Water Goblin* and *The Noon Witch*. What's more, several of the themes, especially in *The Water Goblin* and *The Golden Spinning Wheel*, are conceived as wordless settings of actual lines in Erben's ballads – an innovative procedure which anticipated and influenced Janáček's practice of 'spoken melody' ('nápěvky').

That said, the principal attractions of the Erben symphonic poems tend to be colouristic rather than structural. *The Water Goblin*, for example, is a free rondo in which the goblin's foursquare theme provides cohesion only at the expense of overexposure; but there are memorably touching moments, especially in the sixth episode where, on the girl's return to her mother's cottage, Dvořák conjures an atmosphere at once peaceful yet infused with menace. *The Noon Witch* is perhaps the most tightly structured of the symphonic poems, but here too it is individual episodes that stick in the mind: the quirky domesticity of the opening scene, in which the child's toy cockerel is vividly evoked by a piping oboe; the entry of the witch, where (as in the *Requiem*) Dvořák exploits the sinister potential of the bass clarinet, here heard below skeletal muted strings; and the hair-raising proto-cinematic sweep of the witch's demands for the child. The longest of the symphonic poems, *The Golden Spinning Wheel* is also the least integrated, revealing Dvořák at his most structurally diffuse and his most orchestrally versatile; perhaps appropriately for a tale of mutilation, the work is sometimes performed with cuts suggested by the composer's son-in-law Josef Suk. By contrast, *The Wild Dove* is one of the most transparently structured of the group – Dvořák even numbered its five sections in the score. It is simple to follow the narrative from the uneasy, at times almost Mahlerian, funeral march with which, at the outset, the widow accompanies her husband's body to the grave, through her meeting with the young man (his presence announced by a distant trumpet) and their wedding celebrations (complete with flute-and-oboe bagpipe music), to her ultimate remorse and suicide. The call of the dove, rendered on *tremolando* flute, harp and oboe, opens a window on the uncanny, and its after-warblings permeate the concluding return of the funereal music. The work ends with a hint of redemption, in a passage that surely left its mark on the conclusion of Janáček's opera *The Cunning Little Vixen*. It is perhaps inevitable that such rich and often highly spiced orchestral fare has left some listeners, both at the time and since, with a kind of aesthetic indigestion. Hanslick, for example, unable to reconcile himself to speaking of Dvořák and Richard Strauss in the same breath, issued a 'quiet friendly warning' about the 'slippery slope' down which he saw his friend's music threatening to descend. For Simrock, however, the symphonic poems were perfectly marketable commodities, and he happily offered Dvořák 12,000 marks for the first three.

The Water Goblin, *The Noon Witch* and *The Golden Spinning Wheel* were given a joint premiere by Antonín Bennewitz in front of an invited audience in Prague on 3 June 1896 (the first public performances took place in London in the autumn, with Henry Wood conducting *The Water Goblin* and *The Noon Witch*, and Richter conducting *The Golden Spinning Wheel*). Indeed, 1896 was a year of first performances. Dvořák had already conducted the premiere of the five orchestrated *Biblical Songs* in Prague's Rudolfinum on 4 January at the inaugural concert of the Czech Philharmonic Orchestra – the independent reincarnation of the National Theatre Orchestra in which he had worked for so many years as an unknown viola player. On 16 February he attended the Vienna premiere of the 'New World' Symphony, which was conducted by Richter and proved his greatest ever success in the Austrian capital: he sat with Brahms in the director's box and was repeatedly called to acknowledge applause between movements, descending to the platform for a grand ovation at the end of the whole work. Then, on 19 March, Dvořák was in London to conduct the world premiere of the Cello Concerto at a Philharmonic Society concert in the Queen's Hall. The run-up to the concert was fraught with administrative misunderstandings, as a result of which the soloist was not the work's dedicatee, Wihan, but the English cellist Leo Stern. Dvořák had drilled Stern hard to get him up to speed, and the concerto was well received, but this time Dvořák found the scene of his former triumphs rainswept and unpalatable. He was never to return to England.

At the end of March he was in Vienna again to conduct a performance of *The Spectre's Bride*. His visit to Brahms on this occasion may be the one described by Suk, at which Brahms offered to put his own fortune at Dvořák's disposal if he would move to Vienna; but the two men had obviously discussed the matter before, the Vienna Conservatoire having offered Dvořák a professorship at the end of December 1895 on the strength of a groundless rumour that he had agreed to relocate. Suk also recounts how the conversation turned to religion and that Dvořák was deeply disconcerted to realise the depth of Brahms's agnosticism. On the way back from Brahms's house he was even more than usually quiet, finally sighing in incomprehension: 'Such a man, such a soul – and he believes in nothing, he believes in nothing!' Brahms for his part seems never to have found in Dvořák's faith the absurdity he found in some of its tenets, such as the belief in miracles that informs the text of *Saint Ludmila*, and there is humanity and insight in his defence that 'A man so industrious as Dvořák by no means has time to get stuck on doubts; rather all his life he stands by what he was taught in his childhood'.

No such religious differences stood between Dvořák and Anton Bruckner, on whom he also seems to have called during his stay in Vienna in March. Here, if Suk's account of the visit is to be taken at face value, the barrier was rather Bruckner's spiritual abstractedness. On arrival at his vaulted flat in the Schloss Belvedere, they found the septuagenarian composer sitting at his writing desk in his shirtsleeves. He seemed to look through rather than at them and for a long time could not understand that they had come to invite him to a concert at which his String Quintet was to be performed. When he finally grasped their purpose he cried off on the grounds that he was working on his Ninth Symphony:

> When we took our leave, he was suddenly very upset. There were tears in his remarkable eyes. He accompanied us to the door in his quilted waistcoat and waved kisses to us as long as our carriage was in sight.

Little more than six months later Bruckner was dead, leaving his Ninth Symphony as one of the great unfinished masterpieces of the nineteenth century.

Dvořák's first performances that year continued with the Prague premiere of the Cello Concerto, again with Leo Stern as the soloist, on 11 April. Then five days later the first performance of the String Quartet in A flat major was privately given by the ensemble most closely associated with Dvořák and the Czech chamber music repertoire of the second half of the century: the Bohemian Quartet. The Bohemians' cellist, Wihan (whose pupils, including Suk, were the quartet's founding members), clearly bore the composer no ill will at his displacement from the London and Prague premieres of the Cello Concerto, and it was the Bohemian Quartet who gave the first public performance of the G major quartet too, in Prague on 9 October.

Around the time of this premiere Dvořák heard on the grapevine that Brahms was seriously ill. For reasons that remain obscure, however, he acted on this knowledge only in March the following year, travelling to Vienna to visit his old friend for what he must immediately have realised was the last time. Brahms died of liver cancer three weeks later, and Dvořák visited Vienna again to attend the funeral; later in the year, with a sort of historical inevitability, he was elected to fill Brahms's empty seat on the jury for the Austrian State Stipendium. In September Dvořák was a mourner at a funeral for another friend, Karel Bendl, his fellow-composer and companion of his youth at the Prague Organ School.

A few months earlier Dvořák had conducted two of the Erben symphonic poems in Brno, kindling Janáček's excitement at what he was to call the most Czech of all Dvořák's works. On 20 March 1898 Janáček expressed his admiration for the older composer by conducting the world premiere of *The Wild Dove* in Brno. At Vysoká later in the year Dvořák started a fifth symphonic poem, *A Hero's Song* ('Píseň bohatrýrská'), Op. 111 (B.199), which was completed by 25 October. Unlike the Erben poems, *A Hero's Song* has no pre-existing programme, but Dvořák outlined to one correspondent the kind of hero he had in mind, providing an interesting insight into the correlative nature of his musical thinking in these late programmatic works:

Naturally I was thinking more of a champion of the spirit, an artist, and I believe I depicted the hero accurately in the first theme. This theme is full of energy, resolution and power... In

the second theme ... in B flat minor, sorrow, lamentation, etc.
are expressed for the first time in conflict with D flat major,
which symbolises hope and consolation. Fresh joy and hope for
a happier future are introduced in the E major 2/4 section...
and at the end great turbulence leads to ultimate victory for
the spiritual and artistic ideal...

Dvořák's heroic mode can tend towards the bombastic, especially when developed at such length, but just as the Erben poems had found a champion in Janáček, so *A Hero's Song* was taken up by the thirty-eight-year-old Gustav Mahler, who had recently added the conductorship of the Vienna Philharmonic to his directorship of the Vienna Court Opera. It was Mahler who gave the premiere of the new work in the Austrian capital in December 1898. Despite such august adherents, however, *A Hero's Song* remains an anticlimactic conclusion to Dvořák's magnificent career as an instrumental composer.

If Hanslick had been worried by the Straussian tendencies in Dvořák's Erben-inspired symphonic poems, he must have seen his 'friendly warning' as uncomfortably close to prophecy when, a year after *A Hero's Song*, Richard Strauss himself produced *Ein Heldenleben* ('A Hero's Life'). Dvořák seems to have lost little sleep over such criticism, however. Ever since the United States had provided him with financial security, he had made it clear that he was going to write not what people expected of him but what he wanted to write. And what he wanted to write now was what he had always most wanted to write: with the exception of two minor vocal works, the remainder of his creative career would be given over to opera.

Dvořák had recast *Dimitrij* along Wagnerian lines in 1894, and throughout 1897 he had been working on a thoroughgoing revision of *The Jacobin*; but it was a decade since he had completed an original opera. By the time the revised *Jacobin* received its first performance at the National Theatre on 18 June 1898, however, he was already six weeks into work on *The Devil and Kate* ('Čert a Káča'), the first of three stage works which would represent the final flowering of his lifelong operatic ambitions.

The Devil and Kate, Op. 112 (B.201) belongs to the same world as the Erben symphonic poems. As with so many of his earlier operas, Dvořák's librettist was a non-professional writer, in this case Adolf Wenig, a young schoolmaster who was the nephew of the Director of the National Theatre, František Adolf Šubert. The story on which Wenig drew was a familiar Czech folk-tale. Kate is a talkative soul who cannot find a lover among the village lads. When no one will dance with her at a local fair she announces in a fit of pique that she would dance with the devil himself if he appeared. Cue Marbuel, who sings a seductively sinister advertisement for the 'scarlet splendour' in which he lives and to which he snatches Kate away. The scene shifts to hell, a region seemingly as much nightclub as place of eternal punishment. Here Kate's garrulity drives the devil mad and Marbuel hatches a plan with Jirka the shepherd, who dances her out of the nether world in what, especially after the Slavonic gusto of the devils' dance a few moments earlier, seems a rather perfunctory manner. The final act is a tailpiece to the main plot, in which a local princess is saved from damnation because Marbuel cannot face meeting Kate again. The opera is a curious but attractive conflation of the Wagnerian procedures of Dvořák's last years – there are few stand-alone numbers, for example, the action being advanced principally in continuous exchanges of dialogue – and the dance idioms of his first Slavonic period. *The Devil and Kate* was the first of Dvořák's operas to be performed in Britain, in Oxford in 1932.

The pattern of Dvořák's life during the years after his return from America is increasingly that of a man finally able to organise his time in the way he likes, and sufficiently sure of himself to do so in the face of professional temptation. Just as he now wrote only what he felt like writing, so he narrowed down his other musical activities to those that fully engaged his interest. He rejected new approaches from Jeannette Thurber, making it clear that, while he was happy for the National Conservatory to use his name on their notepaper, his days as an executive director were over. He also turned down an invitation from the Philharmonic Society in London and a commission from August Manns for the 1899 Sheffield Music Festival. He spent as much time as possible at Vysoká – a late photograph shows him, white-bearded and corpulent,

Dvořák with his pigeons at Vysoká

179

sitting on the courtyard bench contentedly observing his pigeons – and reduced his travels even to musical centres much closer than London or New York. One such visit was to Vienna in December 1898 to attend Mahler's rehearsals for *A Hero's Song*, where a fly on the wall would have seen two sons of Bohemia – the one notoriously undemonstrative, the other emotionally volatile almost to the point of psychosis – united in pursuit of their common art. Six months later Dvořák was in the imperial capital again, this time to be received by the Emperor himself, who awarded him – an honour almost without precedent for a composer – the prestigious medal *Litteris et Artibus*; Dvořák, true to form, called it his 'big gold plate'. Gratifying as such tokens of recognition undoubtedly were, the real highlights of this period for Dvořák were the double celebration of his own silver wedding anniversary and his daughter Otilie's wedding to Josef Suk on 17 November 1898 (an event to which hundreds of guests were invited from all over Europe), and the completion of *The Devil and Kate* on 27 February 1899. Family and composition remained, as they had always been, the dual core of his life.

The Devil and Kate received its first performance under Adolf Čech at the National Theatre on 23 November 1899 and was as successful as its composer could have wished. Ever since finishing the opera, Dvořák had of course been on the lookout for a new libretto. Only in the spring of 1900, however, did he find a workable one. This was *Rusalka* – effectively a Bohemianisation of Hans Christian Andersen's *Little Mermaid* and related fairytales – by the rising young poet and playwright Jaroslav Kvapil. Like *The Devil and Kate*, the libretto (which had already done the rounds of Suk, Foerster and Nedbal without finding a taker) was brought to Dvořák's attention by Šubert, whose post as director of the National Theatre Kvapil himself would one day hold. It tells the story of a water nymph, Rusalka, who, having fallen in love with a prince, persuades a sorceress to grant her a human body and soul so she can be with him. The sorceress grants her wish, but decrees that Rusalka must remain dumb while in the human world and must suffer eternal damnation if the prince rejects her love. All ends unhappily when the prince jilts her for a cold-hearted princess, only to realise too late that it is Rusalka he really loves. Returning to the water nymph's lake, he begs her to kiss him, even though he knows the kiss will be fatal, and the opera concludes with his death and Rusalka sinking back into the half-life of eternity.

Given Dvořák's immersion in folklore material during these years, this was a match made in heaven. On 4 April he made his last public appearance as a conductor, with the Czech Philharmonic Orchestra. Two weeks later he finished *Festival Song* ('Slavnostní zpěv') for chorus and orchestra, Op. 113 (B.202) to mark the seventieth birthday of Josef Tragy, his former boss at the Prague Conservatoire. Only then was he free to start work on *Rusalka*, and it is an indication of how completely the project had already seized his imagination that the first act was sketched in just over a fortnight. Kvapil described how Dvořák would sometimes turn up at his flat at seven o'clock in the morning, having already completed his round of the Prague railway stations, only to forget why he had come, talk about anything but the opera, then light a cigar and leave. There were no equivalent lapses in his musical concentration, though, and the whole score was completed on 27 November 1900.

Rusalka, Op. 114 (B.203) is the most successful of Dvořák's operas and the only one yet to have established a lasting reputation outside his homeland; indeed, it is one of the best loved of all Czech operas. The subject inspired Dvořák to some of his most ravishing, and at times almost impressionistic, music. There is, in particular, an otherworldly, melancholy luminescence to his scoring for the supernatural characters and settings which bathes not only Rusalka's beautiful Act I song to the moon 'Měsíčku na nebi hlubokém' ('O silver moon') – the opera's best-known piece, often performed as a separate concert item – but also the erotically charged scene in which she describes herself washing against the bathing prince as a wave, the desolation of her lament 'Mladosti své pozbavena' ('My youth is gone') at the beginning of Act III, and the doomed ecstasy of that final kiss. The ambient melancholy embraces even the secondary characters. The Water Goblin, for example, a benevolent relative of the Vodník of Dvořák's symphonic poem, attains a kind of tragic nobility by virtue of his impotent sympathy for Rusalka, and even in the opening scene his wistful aside on the youth of the wood-nymphs ('inu, mladí, mladí') confers a psychological depth unexpected in such an off-the-peg fairytale figure.

The first performance, at the National Theatre on 31 March 1901, was a triumph, and the following morning Dvořák burst into the theatre office in a state of great excitement, demanding a new libretto from Kvapil 'while I am in the mood!' (If he noticed among the rave reviews one scathingly discordant one by a young music critic called Zdeněk Nejedlý, he is unlikely to have paid it much heed. It was, however, the first shot in a long and bitter campaign to canonise Smetana at Dvořák's expense: fifty years later, as Minister of Education and Culture in Communist Czechoslovakia, Nejedlý would elevate his lifelong prejudice against Dvořák to the status of official policy.)

Mahler, his appetite whetted by *A Hero's Song*, was hugely taken with *Rusalka* when he looked through the piano arrangement, and within five weeks of the premiere he approached Dvořák with a view to directing it in German translation at the Vienna Court Opera. Since so much of Dvořák's emotional energy had been invested for so long in securing just such an operatic breakthrough, his delay in reaching agreement remains hard to understand. It was a year before he signed a (very favourable) contract, and this loss of momentum may itself have contributed to the eventual foundering of the project. Given Dvořák's history of ambivalence towards the Viennese stage, who knows what psychological factors may have been at play amid the financial and political wrangling.

1901 was the year of Dvořák's sixtieth birthday, and tributes came thick and fast. In April he was called to the platform with fanfares and ovations when Nikisch, now back in Europe after his time as conductor of the Boston Symphony Orchestra, brought the Berlin Philharmonic to Prague for a concert which included *The Wild Dove*. Around the same time Dvořák was appointed a member of the Herrenhaus, the upper house of the Austrian parliament (analogous to the British House of Lords), together with Jaroslav Vrchlický, his librettist on *Saint Ludmila*. It is testimony to Dvořák's status that his nomination was an act of political appeasement towards Czech opinion inflamed by a recent decree banning the use of the Czech language in local government and the law courts. However, evidence of Dvořák's political sophistication – or lack of it – in this new forum is limited to his taking the oath: his first appearance there on 14 May, wearing morning dress and his 'big gold plate', was also his last. If the press outside were looking for a soundbite, they must have been disappointed. Dvořák seemed most excited by the quality of the pencils provided for the legislators, pocketing the lot to show Anna with the less than immortal words, 'Look at these, they're just the thing for writing music!'

In July he was appointed Director of the Prague Conservatoire in succession to Bennewitz (though, management not being Dvořák's forte, the day-to-day administration was left to a deputy). His birthday month released a damburst of tributes and performances, which lasted for much of the rest of the year and included the staging of six of his operas at the National Theatre, a torchlight procession to his house by members of the Prague Hlalol, and the inevitable banquets and presentations. Dvořák's reaction to this epidemic of national hero-worship can have surprised no one who knew him: 'Is all this really necessary?' He made sure he was out of Prague on his actual birthday, told the revellers outside his flat to keep the noise down, and even skipped *The Cunning Peasant* and *Dimitrij* at the National Theatre.

Perhaps his grumpiness was partly a defence against the sclerotic effect of celebrity. He would not, after all, be the first creative artist to fear that institutional status would suffocate his muse. There is a rare hint of creative insecurity in a letter of February 1902 to Emil Kozánek, the conductor of the National Theatre: 'For more than fourteen months I have done *no work*,' he wrote, 'and been unable to *make up my mind*, and I don't know how long this state of affairs will continue.' As ever, his indecision had to do with opera. Since finishing *Rusalka* in November 1900 he had written only a single short work, *Song from the Blacksmith of Lešetín* ('Zpěv z Lešetínského kováře'; B.204), composed over two days in August 1901. For Dvořák, this was an unprecedented period of creative idleness. As his exhortation to Kvapil shows, however, he had been casting around for a new libretto since at least the morning after the *Rusalka* premiere. He had taken up various candidates and put them aside again, but shortly after writing his letter to Kozánek he finally decided on a libretto written several years earlier by his fellow member of parliament, Vrchlický. This was a treatment of the story of Armida, an episode in Tasso's *Gerusalemma liberata* which had already done service for dozens of opera composers, including Handel, Gluck, Haydn and Rossini. The attraction to Dvořák of this well-worn tale was presumably that it offered the possibility of a more international appeal, but by that very token it was a drastic departure from the distinctive territory of Slavonic folklore marked out by all his works since 1896 and so resoundingly appreciated by the audiences still pouring into performances of *Rusalka*.

Armida occupied Dvořák from 11 March 1902 until 23 August 1903, a far longer gestation than its two predecessors, and one that no doubt reflects some of the difficulties inherent in the libretto's mixture of love story, Christian chivalry and old-fashioned sword-and-sorcery supernaturalism. From the first, the auguries for the premiere were ominous. The conductor Karel Kovařovic seems to have been less than wholehearted about the opera, perhaps because he himself had abandoned work on the selfsame libretto nine years before. The rehearsals were dogged by illness and incompetence, and the first performance had to be postponed. By the time it took place on 25 March 1904, everyone's tempers had been tested to and beyond their limits. Then during the premiere itself, which was conducted by František Picka, Dvořák was taken ill with a sudden pain in his side and had to leave the theatre.

The indisposition saved him from witnessing the audience's response to his last opera, which was no more than a *succès d'estime*, but it seemed to trigger an escalating sequence of ailments over the following weeks. Dvořák's anger when someone suggested the pain might be symptomatic of kidney disease, and the extreme irritability

Janáček noticed during the rehearsals for *Armida*, perhaps indicate a fear that his condition was more serious than the lumbago he claimed it was. Certainly, mortality was much on his mind: his mother-in-law, whose sterling ministrations to the children had made possible his visits to America, had recently died, as had his old friends Antonín Rus and Adolf Čech. In the short term, however, his doctors saw no cause for alarm, and after taking things easy for a few days he felt strong enough to make one of his trainspotting excursions to Vinohrady station. Shortly afterwards he developed flu-like symptoms which kept him in bed for the best part of a month, and were sufficiently alarming on at least one occasion for the doctor to be summoned in the middle of the night. On 1 May, however, Dvořák got up for lunch with his family, took his customary place at the head of the table, and sank a bowl of soup. No sooner had he finished than he complained of dizziness, went pale then purple in the face, and fell back in his chair, struggling to speak. By the time the doctor arrived he was already dead. Retrospective diagnosis is a notoriously inexact science, but it seems likely that the proximate cause of death was a thrombosis induced by his extended confinement to bed. He was sixty-two years old.

Janáček was at a concert in Warsaw when the news filtered through. The programme was changed to include the *Hussite Overture*, and Janáček recorded how afterwards the concertgoers stood in the foyer together in shocked disbelief. At the National Theatre in Prague that evening the audience arriving for a performance of Smetana's *Brandenburgers in Bohemia* found the auditorium draped in black. Dvořák's funeral, on 5 May, was an occasion of national mourning. Tens of thousands stood in silence at the roadside as the cortège processed from St Salvator's church to the National Theatre. Here, at the cultural heart of the Czech nation, the 'Introit' of Dvořák's own *Requiem* was sung from the balcony. Then the solemn procession wound on up the hill to the Vyšehrad cemetery, where the composer took his rightful place among the heroes of the country he loved.

Personalities

Anger, Mořic (1844–1905): Friend and supporter of Dvořák, with whom he briefly shared a flat in Prague. A violinist and fellow member of Komzák's band, he became deputy conductor of the National Theatre Orchestra and gave the premiere of *Dimitrij* in 1882.

Apt, Antonín (1815–1887): Conductor of the St Cecilia Society orchestra, in which Dvořák played viola in his student days. A devotee of Liszt and Wagner, he provided Dvořák with his first taste of the 'new German music' which was to be a lifelong passion.

Bendl, Karel (1838–1897): Bohemian composer of operas and choral works, in his time regarded almost as an equal of Dvořák and Smetana. A close friend of Dvořák from their days at the Prague Organ School, he was co-founder and conductor of the Prague Hlalol, and stood in for Dvořák at the Prague Conservatoire during the latter's residency in the United States.

Brahms, Johannes (1833–1897): German composer, widely seen as Dvořák's greatest contemporary. As a member of the jury for the Austrian State Stipendium, he introduced Dvořák to his own publisher, Simrock, thus giving him his big international break. A selfless promoter of Dvořák and his music thereafter, he and Dvořák became close friends.

Bülow, Hans von (1830–1894): German conductor and pianist. Liszt's son-in-law before his wife Cosima left him for Wagner, Bülow was an immensely influential figure in German music in the second half of the nineteenth century. As conductor of the Berlin Philharmonic from 1887 to 1893, he was a persuasive advocate of Dvořák's music. Dvořák dedicated his Fifth Symphony to him and pasted his picture onto the title page of his Seventh.

Čech, Adolf (1842–1903): Leading Czech conductor and supporter of Dvořák, with whom he shared a desk in the St Cecilia Society orchestra. As conductor of the National Theatre Orchestra, he gave several premieres of Dvořák's works, including the Sixth Symphony in 1881 and *The Jacobin* in 1889.

Červinková-Riegrová, Marie (1854–1895): Czech writer. The daughter of the leading nationalist politician František Ladislav Rieger, she provided two of Dvořák's most successful libretti, for the operas *Dimitrij* and *The Jacobin*. Her father introduced Dvořák to Tchaikovsky in 1888.

Dvořák, František (1814–1894): The composer's father. A failed butcher-cum-innkeeper, he became in later years a professional zither player. There is no evidence to support the legend that he tried to force his son to follow the family trade.

Dvořáková, Anna (*née* Čermáková) (1854–1931): Dvořák's wife and mother of his six surviving children. The younger sister of the composer's first love, Josefina, she was an accomplished contralto in her own right and an able business manager for her husband.

Ehlert, Louis (1825–1884): Influential German music critic and composer, whose glowing 1878 review of the *Slavonic Dances*, Op. 46 and the *Moravian Duets*, Op. 32 in the Berlin *Nationalzeitung* introduced Dvořák to a German-speaking audience and transformed his fortunes.

Erben, Karel Jaromír (1811–1870): Czech poet and folklorist, whose 1853 collection *Garland of National Legends* provided the source for Dvořák's cantata *The Spectre's Bride* and the symphonic poems *The Water Goblin*, *The Noon Witch*, *The Golden Spinning Wheel* and *The Wild Dove*.

Fibich, Zdeněk (1850–1900): The most eminent Czech composer of his time after Dvořák and Smetana, he was deputy conductor and choirmaster of the Provisional Theatre from 1875 to 1881. His symphonic poems anticipate those of Dvořák's final years. He is best known today for his opera *Šárka* and his numerous short piano pieces *Moods, Impressions and Reminiscences* ('Nálady, dojmy a upomínky').

Foerster, Josef Bohuslav (1859–1951): Czech composer of operas, symphonies, concertos, chamber works and songs, and one of Dvořák's most eminent contemporaries. His father Josef taught at the Prague Organ School when Dvořák was a student there, and his wife, the soprano Berta Foerstrová-Lauterová, sang in the premiere of *The Jacobin*.

Göbl, Alois (1841–1907): A lifelong friend of Dvořák, he trained as a singer but gave up a musical career to become a teacher and administrator on Prince Rohan's estate at Sychrov in Bohemia, where Dvořák often visited him. He was one of few correspondents with whom Dvořák discussed his compositions while he was working on them.

Hálek, Vítězslav (1835–1874): Czech poet and dramatist. Dvořák's setting of his patriotic poem *Heirs of the White Mountain* provided the composer with his first great public success in 1873. Hálek also wrote the lyrical poems Dvořák set in his *Evening Songs*, Op. 3 in 1876.

Hanslick, Eduard (1825–1904): Highly influential Czech-born music critic, based in Vienna. As a member of the jury for the Austrian State Stipendium, he introduced Dvořák to Brahms and became a strong supporter of Dvořák's music. He was a fierce opponent of Liszt and Wagner and a committed advocate for the 'absolute music' of Brahms.

Janáček, Leoš (1854–1928): Moravian composer and Dvořák's most eminent Czech successor. A lifelong friend and walking companion of Dvořák, whose music he promoted in Brno and who influenced his own development, he wrote critical assessments of the late symphonic poems and gave the premiere of *The Wild Dove*. Most of the works by which he is now known were written after Dvořák's death.

Joachim, Joseph (1831–1907): Hungarian-born violinist, based in Germany, and one of the greatest virtuosos of his time. Introduced to Dvořák by Brahms, he was the dedicatee of Dvořák's Violin Concerto and, as founder of the Joachim Quartet, an influential exponent of Dvořák's string quartets.

Komzák, Karel (1823–1893): Czech bandleader and composer. From 1859 Dvořák was principal viola in his private orchestra, which became the nucleus of the National Theatre Orchestra in 1862. In 1865 Komzák's band was formally subsumed into the National Theatre Orchestra, in which Dvořák played until 1871.

Kounicová, Josefina (*née* Čermáková) (1849–1895): Dvořák's sister-in-law and first love, whom he met as his piano pupil in 1865. A successful actress, she married Count Václav Kounic (Kaunitz) in 1877, and Vysoká, where they had their estate, became the Dvořák family's summer home. The Cello Concerto, written during her last illness, contains references to one of her favourite songs.

Kovařík, Josef Jan (1870–1951): American-born violinist who studied at the Prague Conservatoire, he was a travelling-companion-cum-general-factotum to Dvořák during the composer's first residency in the United States. Spillville, Iowa, where Dvořák spent his first summer in America, was Kovařík's home village.

Krehbiel, Henry Edward (1854–1923): The doyen of American music critics, Krehbiel was the critic for the *New York Tribune* during Dvořák's time in the United States and one of the most thoughtful analysts of his music. Dvořák discussed the 'New World' Symphony with him in uncharacteristically open fashion.

Krejčí, Josef (1822–1881): Principal of the Prague Organ School from the second year of Dvořák's studies there, in succession to the more conservative Karel Pitsch (1786–1858). Subsequently director of the Prague Conservatoire, he was the dedicatee of Dvořák's First String Quartet in A major, Op. 2.

Kvapil, Jaroslav (1868–1950): Czech poet, who provided the libretto for Dvořák's most successful opera, *Rusalka*, and later became director of the National Theatre.

Lachner, Ferdinand (1856–1910): Violinist and the third member of the trio formed by Dvořák and the cellist Hanuš Wihan for Dvořák's farewell tour of Bohemia before his departure for the United States in 1892.

Liehmann, Antonín (1808–1879): A schoolteacher and composer, Liehmann gave Dvořák his first formal instruction in music, at Zlonice from 1853 to 1855, for which the composer remained grateful for the rest of his life. The character of Benda in *The Jacobin* (the archetype of the Bohemian Kantor) is a tribute to Liehmann.

Littleton, Alfred (1845–1914): English music publisher. The son of Henry Littleton, the sole owner of the publishers Novello, Ewer and Co., whom he succeeded on the latter's death in 1888, Alfred Littleton was crucially instrumental in the success of Dvořák's English tours. He also acted as middleman between Jeannette Thurber and Dvořák in negotiating the composer's American contract.

Littleton, Henry (1823–1888): English music publisher. As sole owner of Novello, Ewer and Co., he was a key figure in the organisation and success of Dvořák's earlier English tours. Novello became Dvořák's favoured English publisher and the composer often stayed at Littleton's house in Sydenham on his visits to the United Kingdom.

Mahler, Gustav (1860–1911): Bohemian-born Austrian composer and conductor. A supporter of Dvořák's music, he gave the premiere of the symphonic poem *A Hero's Song* with the Vienna Philharmonic in 1898. As director of the Vienna Court Opera from 1897, he negotiated with Dvořák to stage *Rusalka*, but the performance never took place.

Manns, August (1825–1907): German-born conductor who, as assistant and then principal conductor of the Crystal Palace orchestra from 1854 to 1901, was an active supporter of Dvořák, giving the British premieres of several of his works, including the first of the *Slavonic Dances* to be heard in England.

Maýr, Jan Nepomuk (1818–1888): The first conductor of the National Theatre Orchestra. Dvořák was principal viola under his baton from 1862 (when the Komzák band was conscripted to form the core of the theatre orchestra) to 1866 when Smetana took over the conductorship.

Nedbal, Oskar (1874–1930): Czech composer, conductor and viola player. One of Dvořák's most successful composition students at the Prague Conservatoire, he was also the viola player of the Bohemian Quartet, which did more to promote Czech music in general (and Dvořák's string quartets in particular) than any other chamber ensemble of the time.

Novák, Vítězslav (1870–1949): Czech composer. An important figure in Czech music in the first half of the twentieth century, he was one of Dvořák's star composition students at the Prague Conservatoire. His works include the symphonic poems *In the Tatras* ('V Tatrách') and *About the Eternal Longing* ('O věčné touze').

Ondříček, František (1857–1922): Czech violinist and composer who gave the first performance of Dvořák's Violin Concerto in 1883, and who also performed in the premieres of the Quintet in G major and the Piano Trio in B flat major.

Procházka, Ludevít (1837–1888): Prague lawyer and influential editor of the music journals *Hudební listy* and *Dalibor*. A friend and former pupil of Smetana, he was one of Dvořák's most important early patrons after the composer left the National Theatre Orchestra in 1871.

Richter, Hans (1843–1916): Hungarian-born conductor. A committed Wagnerian, he was one of the most influential musicians of his time, giving the first full performance of *The Ring* at Bayreuth in 1876. As the long-standing conductor of the Vienna Philharmonic, and the director of a series of London concerts (1879–1902), he was an important interpreter of Dvořák's work in the German- and English-speaking worlds.

Seidl, Anton (1850–1898): Hungarian-born conductor. As conductor of the New York Philharmonic Orchestra (1891–1898), he gave the sensational first performance of the 'New World' Symphony at Carnegie Hall in 1893. A passionate Wagnerian from his youth in Bayreuth, his friendship with Dvořák in the United States may have been influential in the composer's return to 'new German' forms from the 1890s.

Simrock, Fritz (1837–1901): German publisher, to whom Brahms introduced Dvořák in 1877. Simrock's publication of the *Moravian Duets* and commissioning of the *Slavonic Dances* transformed Dvořák into an international name, and their relationship, though often troubled, was a cornerstone of the composer's professional life.

Škroup, František (1801–1862): Czech composer. He wrote the earliest Czech opera, *The Tinker* ('Drátenik'), in 1826, as well as the setting of *Where is my homeland?* ('Kde domov můj?'), which became the joint Czechoslovak national anthem in 1918 and the national anthem of the Czech Republic in 1993. Dvořák used Škroup's tune in his overture *My Homeland*.

Smetana, Bedřich (1824–1884): Czech composer often called the 'father of Czech music'. Dvořák played under Smetana's baton in the National Theatre Orchestra before the latter's deafness caused him to retire in 1874, and Smetana took an early interest in Dvořák's music. Dvořák's relations with him were sometimes uneasy, but the Smetana–Dvořák polarity in Czech musical life was substantially fostered after their deaths, when Dvořák's arch-critic Zdeněk Nejedlý became Minister of Education and Culture in Communist Czechoslovakia.

Spitz (Špic), Josef (1809–1866): The schoolteacher, organist and choirmaster at Nelahozeves, he gave the young Dvořák his first piano lessons and involved him in the musical life of the village.

Šubert, František Adolf (1849–1915): Czech dramatist. As director of the National Theatre, he oversaw the production of several of Dvořák's operas. His project for a series of plays on the life of the fifteenth-century reformer Jan Hus led to the commissioning of the *Hussite Overture*.

Suk, Josef (1874–1935): Czech composer and second violin in the Bohemian Quartet. Perhaps Dvořák's most outstanding student at the Prague Conservatoire, he married his teacher's daughter Otilie in 1898 and was one of the leading Czech composers of the post-Dvořák generation. His String

Serenade has always been popular, and his other orchestral works include *Asrael*, *A Summer's Tale* ('Pohádka léta') and *Ripening* ('Zrání'). His grandson Josef Suk (born 1929) is an internationally known violinist.

Tchaikovsky, Pyotr Il'yich (1840–1893): Russian composer. He met Dvořák on visits to Prague in 1888, and became a friend and a keen supporter of his music. Regarded in Prague as a symbol of Slavonic brotherhood, Tchaikovsky was responsible for inviting Dvořák to conduct in Russia in 1890.

Thurber, Jeannette M. (1850–1946): American philanthropist and musical administrator. The wife of a grocery millionaire, Thurber was responsible for setting up the National Conservatory of Music in America, and for persuading Dvořák to become its director from 1892 to 1895.

Vrchlický, Jaroslav (1853–1912): Czech dramatist, who wrote the libretti for Dvořák's oratorio *Saint Ludmila* and his last opera, *Armida*. Vrchlický and Dvořák were made members of the upper house of the Austrian parliament together in 1901.

Wagner, Richard (1813–1883): German composer, whose music influenced Dvořák profoundly, particularly at the beginning and end of his career, and under whose baton Dvořák played in Prague in 1863. Despite his close friendship with Brahms, Dvořák succeeded in navigating the dangerous waters of Wagner–Brahms partisanship and retained support from adherents of both camps.

Wihan, Hanuš (1855–1920): Czech cellist and friend of Dvořák, with whom he and the violinist Ferdinand Lachner toured Bohemia in 1892. The dedicatee of Dvořák's Cello

Concerto, he was instrumental in the founding of the Bohemian Quartet, in which he was for a while the cellist.

Selected Bibliography

Beckerman, Michael, ed., *Dvořák and his World*, Princeton, 1993

Beckerman, Michael, *New Worlds of Dvořák*, New York and London, 2003

Beveridge, David, ed., *Rethinking Dvořák: Views from Five Countries*, Oxford, 1996

Burghauser, Jarmil, *Antonín Dvořák*, Prague, Eng. trans. 1967

Burghauser, Jarmil, *Antonín Dvořák: Thematic Catalogue*, Prague, 2nd ed. 1996

Butterworth, Neil, *Dvořák* ('The Illustrated Lives of the Great Composers'), London, 1984

Clapham, John, *Antonín Dvořák: Musician and Craftsman*, London, 1966

Clapham, John, *Dvořák*, Newton Abbot and London, 1979

Clapham, John, 'Antonín Dvořák' in *The New Grove Late Romantic Masters*, London, 1985

Döge, Karl, Dvořák entry in Stanley Sadie & John Tyrell, eds, *The New Grove Dictionary of Music and Musicians*, London, 2nd ed. 2001

Dvořák, Otakar, ed. Paul Polansky, *Antonín Dvořák, My Father*, Spillville, Iowa, 1993

Honolka, Kurt, trans. Anne Wyburd, *Dvořák*, London, 2004

Hořejš, Antonín, *Antonín Dvořák: The Composer's Life and Work in Pictures*, Prague, 1955

Hughes, Gervase, *Dvořák: His Life and Music*, London, 1967

Layton, Robert, *Dvořák Symphonies and Concertos*, London, 1978

Robertson, Alec, *Dvořák* ('The Master Musicians Series'), London, 1945, rev. ed. 1964

Schönzeler, Hans-Hubert, *Dvořák*, London and New York, 1984

Smaczny, Jan, *Dvořák: Cello Concerto*, Cambridge, 1999

Šourek, Otakar, *Antonín Dvořák: His Life and Works*, Prague, Eng. trans. 1952

Šourek, Otakar, trans. Roberta Finlayson Samsour, *Antonín Dvořák: Letters and Reminiscences*, Prague, 1954

Glossary

Absolute music Music that is not of a narrative or descriptive kind, as against 'programme music' (see below). During Dvořák's lifetime Brahms was seen as the great exponent of absolute music, in contradistinction to Wagner and Liszt. As an admirer of all three composers, Dvořák straddled both camps. Seen principally as a composer of absolute music – symphonies, chamber works, etc. – he aroused critical comment by turning to programme music in his later years.

Appassionato Impassioned.

Arpeggio A chord spread so that the notes are played one after another, usually from the bottom up.

Autograph A composer's original manuscript score. Dvořák's autographs typically end with the words 'Bohu díky': 'Thanks be to God'.

Canon A musical form in which a single theme is played or sung by two or more voices starting one after another, as in the well-known 'round' *Frère Jacques*.

Cantata A sacred or secular work in several movements for accompanied voice or voices. Dvořák's cantatas include the *Hymnus*, the *Stabat mater* and *The Spectre's Bride*.

Cavatina An instrumental piece with the characteristics of a song.

Coda The tailpiece at the end of a sonata-form movement, following the recapitulation.

Concert champêtre	A pastoral instrumental work, originally played outdoors.
Con fuoco	With fire, fierily.
Con moto	With movement.
Con sordino (plural Con sordini)	Played with the mute – in the case of a stringed instrument a small clamp placed across the bridge.
Counterpoint	The playing together of two or more separate horizontal lines of melody. Music in which counterpoint occurs is described as 'contrapuntal'.
Development	The middle section of a sonata-form movement (coming between the exposition and the recapitulation) in which the thematic material of the exposition is developed.
Diminuendo	Getting gradually quieter.
Dumka (plural Dumky)	A form of Ukrainian elegy, characterised by alternating slow and livelier sections, which Dvořak made his own and used in several works, notably including his *Dumky* trio, Op. 90.
Eclogue	Originally applied to a short pastoral poem, the term is also used of a musical piece with a similar character. Dvořak wrote a set of *Eclogues* for piano, Op. 56.
Exposition	The opening section of a sonata-form movement in which the thematic material, typically including two or more 'subjects', is set out and sometimes repeated.

Feroce Fierce.

Fugue A rigorous form of counterpoint in which several musical 'voices' imitate one another, each entering in succession after the first voice has stated the 'subject' or theme.

Furiant A Bohemian dance, the 'swaggerer's dance' (the etymology has nothing to do with rage), characterised by cross-rhythms. It is one of the folk forms most often adapted by Dvořak, as for example in the first of the *Slavonic Dances*, Op. 46, and the scherzo of the Sixth Symphony.

Humoresque A lively or capricious instrumental piece, often with an undercurrent of sadness. The seventh of Dvořak's *Humoresques* for piano is probably the most famous example ever written.

Intermezzo A movement or section that functions as an interlude, originally in an operatic, but by extension instrumental, work.

Kantor A term denoting a schoolteacher who was typically also the local organist and choirmaster. The cornerstone of the Bohemian music-making tradition, the role was immortalised by Dvořak in *The Jacobin* in the character of Benda, a tribute to Antonín Liehmann who taught the composer in his early years.

Leading note The seventh note of the scale, a semitone below the tonic, to which it 'leads'. It is characteristic of the music of Dvořak's American period that the leading note is sometimes flattened.

Leitmotif A musical theme which recurs throughout a work, often used to symbolise a character or idea in an opera. The term was first used in relation to Wagner's operatic technique.

Libretto Literally 'little book', the words of an opera.

Maestoso Majestic.

Mazurka A Polish country dance in triple time, typically with an accent on the second beat.

Modulation The process of moving from one key to another.

Nachtmusik Night music, a serenade.

Oratorio A sacred or secular dramatic work for solo singers, choir and orchestra.

Pentatonic A five-note scale (e.g. the five black notes on the piano that form the opening of Dvořak's famous *Humoresque* in G flat major). Use of melodic material based on the pentatonic scale is typical of much folk music, and in Dvořak's work is especially associated with the music of his American period.

Polka A Bohemian dance in quick duple time. Fibich, Smetana and Dvořák all incorporated the dance into several of their works.

Programme music Music with an underlying programme or narrative, as against 'absolute music' (see above). Dvořák's late symphonic poems are examples.

Recapitulation The section in a sonata-form movement in which the material of the exposition is reprised in amended form. It follows the development section and is sometimes itself followed by a coda.

Rondo A musical form, often used in the last movement of a work, in which a theme stated at the beginning makes repeated appearances, separated by contrasting episodes.

Scherzo Literally 'joke', typically the liveliest (third or second) movement of a symphony, string quartet, piano sonata, etc. Dvořak's scherzos often deploy Slavonic elements.

Skočná A Bohemian leaping dance in duple time.

Sonata form The most characteristic form for an opening movement (and often other movements too) in a Classical sonata, symphony, etc. In its most regular form it consists of three sections: exposition, in which the thematic material is set out; development, in which the exposition's themes are explored and developed; and recapitulation, in which the material of the exposition is reprised in amended form. There may also be a coda to end the movement.

Sousedská A Bohemian dance in triple time, similar to a waltz or minuet.

Stretta Literally 'drawing together', a passage usually towards the end of a work where the musical material accelerates towards a climax.

Symphonic poem An orchestral work in which the music is guided by an underlying programme or concept as much as by purely musical considerations, the symphonic poem, or 'tone poem', is the most characteristic form of 'programme music' and closely associated with the musical ideas of Liszt. Dvořák composed several symphonic poems on his return from America in 1895.

Syncopation   A pattern of emphasis imposed against the natural rhythm of the music, for example by the accenting of weak beats.

Tierce de Picardie   The use of a major third in the concluding chord or chords of a work in a minor key. A device most characteristic of the Baroque period, it was used to great effect by Dvořak at the end of his Seventh Symphony.

Ternary   Having a three-part structure in which the third part is a repeat of the first. Also known as A–B–A form.

Triad   A three-note chord, typically featuring the first, third and fifth notes of the scale; hence 'triadic'.

Trio   Both a work for three instruments and the contrasting middle section of a scherzo.

A Note on Czech Pronunciation

Czech is not a grateful language to the uninitiated, but it is so consistent in its pronunciation that knowledge of a few basic rules can remove much of the surface difficulty:

Czech words are always stressed on the first syllable. An acute accent (čárka) over a vowel indicates a lengthening of the vowel, not stress. In the case of *u*, however, the čárka only appears on initial letters. Elsewhere, it is indicated by a little circle (kroužek): e.g. Martinů.

c is pronounced *ts*, as in 'ca*ts*'
ch is pronounced as in 'lo*ch*'
j is pronounced *y*, as in '*y*ear'
ou is pronounced *oa*, as in 'g*oa*t'

Letters with a little hook (háček) over them are pronounced as follows:
č is pronounced *ch*, as in '*ch*in'
ě is pronounced *ye*, as in '*ye*s'
ň is pronounced *ny*, like the *n* in '*n*ews'
ř is pronounced like the *rge* of 'bou*rge*ois' (with a rolled *r*)
š is pronounced *sh*, as in '*sh*ot'
ž is pronounced *zh*, like the *s* in 'mea*s*ure'

When a háček is used with a lower case *d* or *t*, it is normally represented by a symbol similar to an apostrophe:
ď is pronounced *dy*, like the *d* in '*d*une'
ť is pronounced *ty*, like the *t* in '*t*une'

It is also worth noting that women's surnames usually take the suffix '*ová*'; thus, for example, the composer's wife is properly called Anna Dvořáková.

Annotations of CD Tracks

All works except *Rusalka* may be heard in full by logging onto the website (see page i).

CD 1

1 Serenade in E major, Op. 22 (B.52). **Movement 1: Moderato**

The five-movement Serenade for strings was written in just eleven days in May 1875, a month before the Fifth Symphony, at a time when Dvořák's fortunes had recently received a significant boost from the award of the Austrian State Stipendium. The first of what is effectively a triptych of serenades for different combinations of instruments (the others being the Serenade in D minor, Op. 44, and the Czech Suite in D major, Op. 39), it is also the earliest of his compositions still to be regularly performed today and has become a staple of the string orchestra repertoire. Typical of the work's simplicity of language and directness of appeal, the opening movement is in ternary form, its graceful outer sections framing a slightly jauntier central section. The main theme of the movement returns to magical effect near the end of the work's finale.

2 Symphony No. 5 in F major, Op. 76 (B.54). **Movement 1: Allegro, ma non troppo**

Like the Serenade in E major, the Fifth Symphony belongs to 1875, a creative *annus mirabilis* for Dvořák, during which he also wrote the String Quintet in G major, Op. 77 (B.49), the first set of *Moravian Duets*, Op. 20 (B.50), the Piano Trio in B flat major, Op. 21 (B.51), the Piano Quartet in D major, Op. 23 (B.53) and, astonishingly, the five act grand opera *Vanda*, Op. 25 (B.55). The Fifth is the first of Dvořák's mature symphonies and marks a significant advance on anything he had achieved before. The early Dvořák biographer and scholar Otakar Šourek heard in the symphony's first movement 'the voice of the rustling woods, the song of the birds, the fragrance of the fields; the strong breath of nature rejoicing and a sense of mortal wellbeing'. The pastoral tone is established from the very first bars, in which a triadic melody for two clarinets ripples gently against a background of hushed strings and horns. The movement is in

207

conventional sonata form, and the coda recreates *pianissimo* the atmosphere of the opening, reminiscences of which also colour the conclusion to the whole symphony.

3 String Quartet No. 8 in E major, Op. 80 (B.57). **Movement 1: Allegro**

The String Quartet in E major is the first of Dvořák's seven mature quartets and one of the finest of all his works in the form. It was written between 20 January and 4 February 1876, immediately after the Piano Trio in G minor, Op. 26 (B.56) and a fortnight before he began sketching the *Stabat mater*, Op. 58 (B.71). The elegiac tone of all three works has been seen as reflecting Dvořák's grief at the death of his baby daughter in September the previous year, while he was working on his grand opera *Vanda*. That tone is powerfully evident in the string quartet, the second composition he began after completing the opera. The tightly constructed opening movement is especially striking for the way in which minor modes subvert the E major tonality from the outset.

4 Stabat mater, Op. 58 (B.71). **'Inflammatus et accensus'**

Dvořák's *Stabat mater* is the first great sacred work of Czech music. A thirteenth-century devotional poem attributed to Jacopone da Todi, *Stabat mater* describes the Virgin Mary's vigil at the foot of the cross and has been set by many composers, including Pergolesi, Haydn, Rossini and Verdi. As a profession of faith in the face of parental grief, the work had a personal resonance for Dvořák, who sketched it between 19 February and 7 May 1876 in the aftermath of the death of his baby daughter and returned to it in October 1877 after the consecutive deaths of two other children left him childless; it was completed on 13 November that year. The work is in ten movements the ninth of which (the contralto solo 'Inflammatus et accensus' – an expression of the supplicant's burning desire for salvation) was often performed as a separate concert item during the composer's lifetime. The uncharacteristically Handelian tread of its opening section perhaps contributed to the *Stabat mater*'s popularity in England, where Joseph Barnby's performance of the work at the Royal Albert Hall in 1883 led to the first of Dvořák's triumphant visits to the country in 1884.

5 Serenade in D minor, Op. 44 (B.77). **Movement 2: Minuetto**

Dvořák's second serenade was written in two weeks in January 1878, shortly after Brahms had introduced him to the influential Berlin publisher Simrock. Scored for pairs of oboes, clarinets and bassoons, plus double bassoon, three horns, cello and double bass, it may have been influenced by Dvořák's hearing Mozart's *Gran partita*, K.361 (sometimes inaccurately called the 'Serenade for Thirteen Wind Instruments') in Vienna shortly before it was written. Nowhere is the work's open-air, Bohemian charm more evident than in the second movement, a delightful minuet and trio. The minuet has about it something of the *sousedská*, a waltz-like Bohemian dance, and both it and the pacier trio contain some of the composer's most sublime writing for the winds. Dvořák later dedicated the serenade to Louis Ehlert, the German critic whose review of the *Moravian Duets* and *Slavonic Dances* launched the composer onto the international stage at the end of 1878.

6 String Quartet No. 9 in D minor, Op. 34 (B.75). **Movement 3: Adagio**

The String Quartet in D minor belongs to the same period of Dvořák's life as the *Symphonic Variations*, Op. 78 (B.70) and the *Stabat mater* (B.71), being composed between 7 and 18 December 1877 in the wake of the deaths of two of his children. There are few more intensely felt movements in the whole of Dvořák's output than this haunting *Adagio*, which follows an *Alla polka* second movement (apparently conceived independently of the second-movement polka in Smetana's String Quartet No. 1 'From My Life', composed a year before Dvořák's but first performed privately in 1878 with Dvořák himself on the viola). Announced *con sordini*, the two somewhat Schubertian main themes are related both to each other and to the second subject of the quartet's first movement, which reappears briefly in the coda. The String Quartet in D minor was dedicated to Brahms, to whom Dvořák was introduced shortly before he began it, and in the light of whose comments he revised the work in the spring of 1878.

7 – 8 Slavonic Dances, Op. 46 (B.78). No. 1 in C major & No. 7 in C minor

The first of Dvořák's two sets of *Slavonic Dances* was commissioned by Brahms's publisher Fritz Simrock in the spring of 1878 and transformed Dvořák virtually overnight from a composer known almost exclusively within the Czech lands to one of Europe's most celebrated new talents. The dances, originally written for piano duet but immediately orchestrated by the composer, have remained immensely popular ever since. Dvořák drew on a wide range of traditional dance forms, but while some of the dances contain echoes of existing melodies, the material is all his own: in the apt words of the American journalist James Gibbons Huneker (1857–1921), Dvořák 'never used quotation marks'. The first dance is a positive explosion of orchestral energy, its framing sections having the cross-rhythms characteristic of the *furiant* or 'swaggerer's dance'. The seventh dance is of more mixed parentage, though its principal models would appear to be Moravian. The main theme is first presented by the oboe, with the bassoon taking it up in canon a bar later, one demonstration among many of Dvořák's extraordinary command of orchestral detail in the *Slavonic Dances*.

9 String Quartet No. 10 in E flat major, Op. 51 (B.92)
   Movement 1: Allegro, ma non troppo

The String Quartet in E flat major was written in response to a commission for a 'Slavonic' work from Jean Becker, the leader of the Florentine Quartet, to whom it is dedicated. Unusually for Dvořák, who generally kept Christmas Day for his family, it was begun on 25 December 1878 and finished, after several interruptions to write smaller works, on 28 March 1879. The opening arpeggio passages convey an extraordinary sense of breadth, and the naturalness with which the movement accommodates its polka-like second subject typifies Dvořák's seamless integration of national elements with the language and formal structures of the Viennese Classical tradition. Also typical of many of Dvořák's sonata movements is the fact that the recapitulation begins not with the first subject but with the second, the arpeggio figures returning to provide an ineffable sense of completion in the closing bars.

10 Symphony No. 6 in D major, Op. 60 (B.112)
Movement 3: Scherzo: Furiant: Presto

Dvořák wrote his Sixth Symphony between 27 August and 15 October 1880 at the request of Hans Richter, who had introduced the composer to the Viennese public with a performance of the third *Slavonic Rhapsody*, Op. 45 (B.86/3) the previous year. It is arguably the most Brahmsian of Dvořák's symphonies, with Brahms's Second Symphony often being cited as a particularly strong influence. There is no mistaking the composer of this full-bloodedly Czech scherzo, however. With its energetic cross-rhythms and relentless forward drive, it is one of Dvořák's most impressive *furiants*. The contrasting trio section, which includes an unusually prominent role for the piccolo, provides an interlude of tranquillity before the *furiant* strikes up again. This is another movement that marries Slavonic and Viennese Classical idioms to entirely personal and wholly convincing effect.

CD 2

1 Piano Trio No. 3 in F minor, Op. 65 (B.130). Movement 1: Allegro ma non troppo

The Piano Trio in F minor was written between 1 February and 31 March 1883 at a time of great soul-searching for Dvořák as he tried to reconcile the conflicting demands of his national and international aspirations. The music's fusion of emotional intensity and intellectual rigour is unprecedented in his output, perhaps also reflecting his grief at the death of his mother some six weeks before he began work on it. The first movement, like the trio as a whole, is conceived on an almost symphonic scale, while retaining all the intimacy of chamber music, and derives much of its motive power from the hushed, jagged theme which the violin and cello announce in bare octaves at the outset. The trio is often seen as marking the beginning of a new phase of Dvořák's creative life, in which Slavonic elements recede under the influence of a more universal musical language.

2️⃣ Symphony No. 7 in D minor, Op. 70 (B.141). **Movement 1: Allegro maestoso**

'I have been engaged on the new symphony for a long, long time,' Dvořák wrote to his publisher Simrock in February 1885; 'after all it must be something really worthwhile, for I don't want Brahms's words to me, "I imagine your symphony quite different from this one (the D major)" to remain unfulfilled.' The Seventh Symphony, which occupied him from 13 December 1884 to 17 March 1885 is indeed strikingly different not only from the Sixth Symphony but from almost everything else Dvořák had written up to that point, only the Piano Trio in F minor, Op. 65 (B.130) approaching the tragic intensity of its language. The principal theme of the opening *Allegro maestoso*, announced *pianissimo* in violas and cellos, conjures an atmosphere of foreboding never fully dispelled in the course of a movement which passes through defiance to resignation and represents one of Dvořák's most tensile musical arguments. Several critics have drawn attention to the similarity between the B flat major second subject and the cello theme in the *Andante* of Brahms's Second Piano Concerto. The symphony is widely regarded as Dvořák's greatest and as one of his finest works in any genre.

3️⃣ Piano Quintet in A major, Op. 81 (B.155)
Movement 3: Scherzo (Furiant): Molto vivace

The Piano Quintet in A major was composed between 18 August and 3 October 1887 and is one of Dvořák's most characteristic chamber works. He was spurred to write it by revisiting the score of the Piano Quintet in A, Op. 5 (B.28), completed fifteen years earlier when he was just beginning to be known in Prague as a composer. His attempts to revise the older work left him unsatisfied, and he composed the new quintet in the same key instead. Although Dvořák designated this effervescent scherzo a *furiant*, it is far from typical of the dance form – a salutary reminder that, while Dvořák was steeped in the folk traditions of the Czech lands, he was always less interested in musicological accuracy than in musical effect. The trio section, marked *Poco tranquillo*, is unusual in using a stripped-down version of the theme of the scherzo itself, introducing the note of melancholy that is seldom far from the surface of the quintet.

[4] Dumky (Piano Trio No. 4 in E minor), Op. 90 (B.166).

Movement 3: Andante – Vivace non troppo

The *Dumky* trio is one of Dvořák's most original creations and has always been among his most popular chamber works. *Dumky* is the plural of *dumka*, a form of Ukrainian elegy characterised by alternating slow and lively sections that Dvořák used in several works, including the String Sextet in A major, Op. 48 (B.80) and the String Quartet No. 10 in E flat, Op. 51 (B.92) (though at least one story suggests that Dvořák was somewhat hazy about the exact definition of the term). The trio was completed on 12 February 1891 and consists of six thematically unconnected movements. The third movement is the culmination of the first part of the work (the first three movements being played without a break) and is one of Dvořák's most haunting inspirations. The fast central section is framed by two melancholy outer sections, a recurrent feature of which is a limpidly beautiful progression of two downward-swooping three-note phrases.

[5] Symphony No. 9 in E minor, Op. 95 (B.178) 'From the New World'

Movement 2: Largo

The 'New World' Symphony, written between 10 January and 24 May 1893, was the first major composition of Dvořák's residency in the United States. It was given a triumphant premiere at Carnegie Hall in December the same year and quickly established itself as one of the composer's most popular works and one of the best-known symphonies in the repertoire. There has been much discussion, fuelled by Dvořák's own comments to the American press, of the extent to which the symphony draws on African-American or Native American sources. Certainly the main cor anglais theme of the slow movement (ushered in by what is, for Dvořák, an unusually harmonically adventurous sequence of chords) has many of the characteristics of a spiritual, and was in fact turned into one in 1922 by one of Dvořák's students, William Arms Fisher, under the title 'Goin' home'. Later in the movement there is a stormy interruption when the motto theme from the first movement appears in the brass in counterpoint with the cor anglais theme. Dvořák described the *Largo* as a sketch

213

for a longer work based on Longfellow's *Hiawatha*, an abortive opera project of his American years.

6 String Quartet No. 12 in F major, Op. 96 (B.179) 'The American'
Movement 2: Lento

At the end of his first academic year in America Dvořák and his family took a three-month holiday in the prairie village of Spillville in Iowa, a Czech settlement which was the family home of the composer's companion and secretary during his first American residency, Josef Jan Kovařík. This was Dvořák's happiest period in the United States, and almost as soon as he arrived in Spillville in June 1893 he started work on what has come to be known as 'The American' Quartet. The work was sketched in just three days and completed less than two weeks later. 'Few people and a great deal of empty space,' is how he described the prairie in a letter home to a friend, and there is a sense of both the expansiveness and the oppressiveness of that unfamiliar landscape in the quartet's haunting slow movement. Untypical of Dvořák's string quartets though it is in many respects, 'The American' remains the most frequently performed of all his works in the form.

7 Humoresques, Op. 101 (B.187). **No. 7 in G flat major: Poco lento e grazioso**

In June 1894, at the end of his first residency in the United States, Dvořák returned to his beloved summer home at Vysoká in southern Bohemia. Back on his native soil for the first time in almost two years, between 7 and 27 August he composed a set of eight *Humoresques* for piano, initially intending them as a set of Scottish dances. Several of these exquisitely crafted miniatures use themes from the composer's American sketchbooks. The seventh piece, with its delicate tripping theme and darker-hued central section, rivals the *Largo* of the 'New World' Symphony for the accolade of Dvořák's best-known composition and has been arranged for many different combinations of instruments.

214

⑧ Cello Concerto No. 2 in B minor, Op. 104 (B.191)
   Movement 3: Finale: Allegro moderato – Andante – Allegro vivo

Despite claiming to dislike the cello as a solo instrument, Dvořák in fact wrote two concertos for it, the first a youthful work from 1865 which remained in short score. The Cello Concerto in B minor is the last composition of Dvořák's American years and is widely regarded as the greatest concerto for its instrument ever written. Composed between 8 November 1894 and 5 February 1895, it has been seen as one of Dvořák's most personal works because of its association with his sister-in-law and first love Josefina Kounicová (*née* Čermáková). On learning that Josefina was seriously ill back home in Bohemia, Dvořák included in the second movement a reminiscence of one of her favourite songs, 'Leave me alone' from his *Four Songs*, Op. 82 (B.157). Shortly after he returned from the United States for the last time, Josefina died, and Dvořák rewrote the coda of the finale to include a further reference to the song. The finale is in free rondo form, and also includes in its closing pages a reminiscence of the theme of the concerto's first movement. The concerto was dedicated to Dvořák's friend the cellist Hanuš Wihan.

⑨ Rusalka, Op. 114 (B.203). Act I: 'O silver moon'

In his last years, Dvořák dedicated himself entirely to the composition of operas, which had always been central to his musical thinking. His penultimate opera, *Rusalka*, was written between 21 April and 27 November 1900 and tells the unhappy story of a water nymph who falls in love with a human prince. Dvořák's only opera to have found a regular place in the repertoire outside the Czech lands, it also contains, in Rusalka's Act I song to the moon 'Měsíčku na nebi hlubokém' ('O silver moon') one of the best loved of all the composer's songs. The water nymph, unable as an incorporeal being to make her love known to the prince, petitions the all-seeing moon to convey her feelings to him as he sleeps.

215

Index

Also Available

Mozart

Beethoven

Chopin

Mahler

Tchaikovsky

Wagner

Puccini